Dedication

To my husband Paul—thank you for your support, encouragement and most of all your understanding, whether I am making art late into the night or arriving home with a new stray cat.

And to my parents—thank you for always encouraging the artist in me. Even if it meant living with crayon on your walls and furniture.

Acknowledgments

My heartfelt thanks goes to F+W Publications for the opportunity to write a second book. I would like to thank my editor Tonia Davenport for all her creative ideas, hard work and encouragement. Also thank you to designer Stephanie Goodrich, photographer Christine Polomsky, Tricia Waddell and the many other people along the way who have made this book a joy to work on and something that I am truly proud of.

TABLE OF CONTENTS

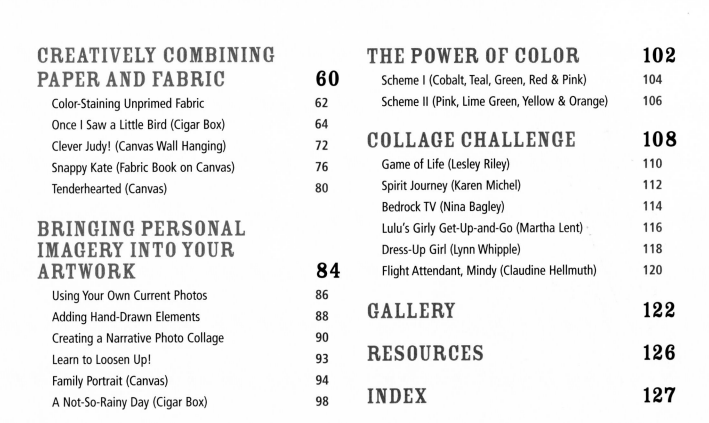

Tom liked his prize

Talk, gossip, speculation

BINGO

BINGO

GET READY TO
STRETCH YOUR IMAGINATION,
MIX THINGS UP
AND EMBARK ON ANOTHER
ARTISTIC ADVENTURE.

I will help you expand your horizons, put more of your personality into your collages and make the whole experience stimulating and fun.

The techniques that I will share with you include: creating crackle paint effects with Elmer's Glue-All, using masking tape as an antique surface treatment and even using dishwasher rinse aid to create a weathered paint look! We'll be working on a variety of surfaces, from altered books and journals to cigar boxes, and from fabric and paper to stretched canvas.

I will show you simple and whimsical ways to add hand-drawn elements to your artwork that will not only be fun and easy to do, but will also give a personal touch to your collage.

You'll learn how a pasta machine can be transformed into a printing press, then how to print onto fabric, glass and paper. I'll show you how to use photos of your children, friends and even pets to add whimsy and intimacy to your collages.

Best of all, these techniques are very versatile. They can be incorporated into your personal collage style—whimsical or serious, romantic or vintage.

No matter what your preference, you'll be able to combine the techniques to create unlimited results!

Developing Your Personal Style

At my workshops, the question, "How do I discover my own personal, artistic style?" is frequently asked. So just how does an artist find their personal style?

There are many ways that artists might find their way to their own approach. I have a process that has helped me and maybe it will work for you.

You'll need to dig deep and discover what it is that you really enjoy about creating art. It might not be what you think it is! It might even mean a change of direction from your current work.

TIME TO CHANGE

Sometimes it's time to shake things up, so, out with the old and in with the new!

After almost a full year of artist's block, my collage-making style took an abrupt turn. What signaled the change was the realization that I was in a rut. I had become too familiar with the way that I had worked in collage for many years and nothing was a surprise anymore. Do you know that feeling? I knew my work needed revitalizing and that it might take drastic measures. My quandary was how to find the excited and energetic feeling that I used to have for creating my artwork.

MAKE LISTS

I began by making lists of the types of artworks that I enjoyed from magazines and galleries. I looked for anything that gave me a "yummy feeling in my tummy," and wrote it down. It was interesting to see how my aesthetic was changing. I found I was drawn to artworks that I previously might not have liked at all. After making many lists, I reviewed what I had written and reduced it to essential concepts: painterly texture, line, whimsical themes, bright colors and drawing.

EXPERIMENT

After I had a list of the concepts I wanted to bring to my artwork, the big question was, "How to begin?" I began experimenting by using inexpensive white paper, crayons, glue stick, a few collage elements, and a pen. I wanted to use simple materials. That way I wouldn't feel pressure to create something "good." I reminded myself that it was "only paper" and I didn't have to show anyone if I didn't want to. I decided to create at least one small collage a day and see where it would lead me. I wanted to make numbers of mini-artworks quickly so that I could create without too much right-brained thinking. The only way to grow is to make a lot of art, so I leapt in!

After a couple of months working this way, I felt I was really onto something. I was excited about my work again. I was giggling and laughing while creating—always a good sign!

IT'S ALL IN A NAME

After my new work had found its footing, I felt like I should give it a name. I thought the name should be a little silly and unusual. I decided to call them "Poppets." My English grandma used the word "poppet" as a term of endearment, frequently telling me "Don't worry, little poppet, everything is going to be okay." Since these new artworks made me feel good, safe and young, the name fit perfectly.

The new direction that my creative style has taken, came from a desire to bring laughter back into my artwork and my life, and it worked.

TAKE YOUR OWN JOURNEY

You can begin your own journey to find an artistic voice by researching artworks and making lists of what inspires you. If you are working from magazines, it's important to use sources

that have a variety of different types of art in them. You don't want to end up looking at artwork that all has the same style. When you come across a piece you enjoy, make notes of what you like about it. Try to be specific and break it down to key elements: line, color, shapes, texture, theme, etc. That way you will extract from the piece the essence of what you really enjoy and you won't risk copying the artist, or duplicating their work directly.

Once you have your list of inspirational concepts, begin by creating at least one small artwork a day. Try to work quickly without thinking about what you should or shouldn't be doing. Enjoy the process and notice how you feel when you are working. Are you excited? Good! If not, maybe you're thinking too hard about it. Keep in mind the key inspirational elements that you gleaned from your research. Use the print-making and background techniques in the following chapters as jumpstarts to creating work in your vision. If it makes you feel looser, try working with inexpensive materials, such as canvas pad or watercolor paper instead of stretched canvas—so that you don't feel inhibited. See where it leads you! Don't edit or judge your work at this time.

JOURNAL AND REVIEW

After about a month of working, lay out your mini-artworks and look at them together. Make notes about what you like and what you'd like to see more of. Color? Line? Themes? You're on your way to discovering your artistic voice! It's very exciting stuff, so let's get started!

Tools and Supplies

There are so many different types of art mediums and surfaces that you can use to create collage, and all of the techniques used in this book will work on just about anything. As a foundation, stretched canvas is nice because it is sturdy and will hold up to many layers of working and reworking. Other surfaces that you can use are: Altoids tins, journal covers, altered books, cigar boxes, canvas pad, wooden shrines from your craft store, and papier-mâché boxes. You name it!

PRESTRETCHED CANVASES

As the name implies, these canvases come already primed and are ready to go out of the package. They are made in just about every size imaginable. You can find several brands, sizes and shapes at craft and art supply stores.

UNPRIMED, UNSTRETCHED CANVAS

Sometimes I prefer unstretched and unprimed fabric and canvas. I like the frayed edges and raw look you can get. You can purchase unprimed canvas from your art supply or fabric stores. Look for cotton duck canvas.

CANVAS PAD

I like to use Fredrix canvas pad for experimenting with techniques that I might cut up and collage with later. It is a pad of individual preprimed canvas sheets. The pads come in sizes from 9" × 12" (23cm × 30cm) to 16" × 20" (41cm × 51cm). It is durable and you can sand on it or sew through it. Many of my students prefer it because it feels less intimidating than working on stretched canvas. In the technique demonstrations in the first part of this book, you'll see I am using sheets of canvas pad cut to approximately 5" × 7" (13cm × 18cm).

WATERCOLOR PAPER

The watercolor paper that I generally use is inexpensive 120-lb (54kgm) paper that comes in a pad of about 10 sheets. There are many different types of watercolor papers and brands—experiment to find what works best for you!

PALETTE PAPER

I prefer to use disposable palette paper for acrylic paints and also for some of the xerographic techniques. It is similar to wax paper but it is sturdier, and each sheet has one waxed and one matte side. It makes clean up easy!

ACRYLIC PAINTS

My favorite acrylic paints to work with are made by Golden Artist Colors, Inc. I enjoy working with the fluid acrylics when I need watery or thinner paint consistency. The heavy-bodied (tube or jar) acrylics are saved for general work and texture building. You might find that the fluid acrylics work best for some of the techniques in this book, because they are thinner and easier to spread. If you have the heavy-bodied, tube acrylics, adding a touch of water will do the trick!

GEL MEDIUM

All my collage work is created with gel medium; it is the only "glue" that I use. I prefer a matte look, so I work with Golden Gel Medium Matte. It comes in a variety of weights from regular to heavy, and finishes such as gloss, semi-gloss and matte. I use the regular weight for general paper gluing and the heavy weight for assemblage and object gluing. It's more archival than an epoxy-type of glue because it will remain flexible and will keep your precious object glued down. Also it won't crack off, cloud or change color over time.

GESSO

Acrylic gesso can be used as a primer for your work surface. If you are working in an altered book or on a cigar box, you might want to give it a coat of gesso before starting, as a primer. A store-bought, stretched canvas or canvas board, it is already primed so you do not need to use gesso before beginning your artwork.

OIL PAINTS

You will need oil paints for the printmaking techniques in this book. Be careful *not* to get the water-soluble oil paints because they won't work! Get good, old-fashioned oils. You can find oil paints at craft stores and at all art supply stores.

WATER-SOLUBLE OIL PASTELS

I prefer to use the Portfolio brand of water-soluble oil pastels, made by Crayola. You can find these at office supply, craft and art supply stores. The Portfolio brand is soft and buttery, and very inexpensive. You can add water to them to make them spread like watercolors.

MARKERS

I have fallen in love with fine-point Permapaque pigment markers to use for color detail on my artworks. They are archival, come in a variety of colors, and they can write over any color background.

FINE-POINT TECHNICAL PENS

I use a variety of fine-point technical pens for linework. Each pen has its own feel and you will want to experiment with what works best for you. Pens that I like to use are: Coptic marker in black .3mm nib and Rotring rapidograph pens in .25mm and .5mm nibs. I often use a fine-tip Sharpie for sketch work or quick drawings.

GUM ARABIC

Gum arabic (a water-soluble gum derived from the Acacia tree), is used as a binder in most watercolor paints. For the techniques in this book, we'll be using it as a printmaking medium. It is nontoxic and I prefer to rub it into the copies with my bare hands, but if you have sensitive skin, use latex gloves. You can find gum arabic in the watercolor paint aisle at your craft or art supply store.

LINSEED OIL

Linseed oil is used to improve the flow and reduce the consistency of oil paints. I use it for xerographic printing techniques because it makes it easier for the paint to release from the copy paper. There are many kinds of linseed oils: refined, purified, etc. For the purposes in this book, any of them will work. I usually buy the refined linseed oil and it works great.

BRUSHES

I buy inexpensive brushes because I usually don't treat them properly. I have found that Loew-Cornell brushes are perfect for me. They have a range of good and expensive brushes, but it's their lower-priced ones that grab my attention. I prefer to use the #1801 set of twelve flat bristle brushes which come in assorted sizes from nos. 1–12. This gives me a range of brushes to use that won't lose their hairs in my artwork and are also inexpensive so when I need to throw them away I don't feel guilty!

PASTA MACHINE

We'll be using a pasta machine as a printmaking press later on in the book. If you wish to try this technique, *don't* reuse it for pasta! You can usually find pasta machines at thrift stores and garage sales.

BRAYER

I find the Speedball 2" (5cm) soft rubber brayer applies paint smoother than a hard plastic brayer. You might want to experiment to see which one you like better.

TAPE

For various projects, you'll need to have regular old masking tape on hand. I don't use any special brand, just whatever is in the office supply aisle when I go grocery shopping or what I find at the hardware store. Try getting a variety of widths and sometimes you can even find tape in different colors.

CLEAR CONTACT PAPER

You'll need a roll of contact paper or shelf-liner paper for one of the background techniques that I will share with you. I use clear contact paper but it doesn't matter if it has a pattern.

FABRIC

I enjoy using various types of fabric in my collages. Since I don't usually need a full yard for my purposes, I often buy "quarter flats" or "quarter rounds" from the fabric stores. This way I get just enough for my collages! You can find fabric at craft stores as well as in traditional fabric stores.

RIBBON

A quick and easy way to finish off your stretched canvas is to glue ribbon to the edge. I buy grosgrain ribbon because I like the texture. Look for a width that's very close to the width of your canvas.

OLD BOOKS

You might want to use an altered book or journal as your art-making surface. I have done this for some of my artworks in this book. You can look for old books at flea markets, garage sales, or libraries. Just about any book will do.

CIGAR BOXES

The cigar boxes that I generally like to use are made of balsa wood and covered with paper. I prefer these because I can leave the lid on or remove it altogether. Usually you can find empty cigar boxes at local wine/spirits stores. Sometimes they will give them to you for free or charge a minimal fee.

OTHER MATERIALS

There are several other items that you will want to have on hand for creating your collage pieces. You probably already have most of the items on this list.

- kneaded eraser
- decorative hole punches
- plastic wrap
- heat gun, embossing type tool or hair dryer
- paper towels
- water jar
- scissors
- craft knife
- photocopies
- spray bottle for water
- waxed paper
- embroidery thread
- needle and sewing thread
- buttons and other sewing notions
- assorted ephemera

Collage Creation Tips

Collage is a wonderful medium because you can create all kinds of images, from funky to serious, or from romantic to silly. When selecting items for collage, I gather a variety of photos and images. Generally, I use antique images of people whom I don't know and create a story about them. These are cast-off photos from times gone by and I imagine I am giving them new life.

PREPARING COPIES OF PHOTOS FOR COLLAGE

When creating images for collage, I prefer to make a copy of the original photo onto white paper. I like the contrast that this gives the photos and because it is black and white, it gives me freedom over what colors I can use for a background. I also enjoy adding text to the torso of the person whom I am collaging. It helps to define the figure and lends interest to the image. The torso text also tells the "story" of the person, as if he or she is wearing their biography.

ONE
Tear Off Some Text

To prepare a figure for collage, start with a photocopy and a passage of text from a book. Tear a line along the top of the section of text you wish to use to create a soft edge.

TWO
Make a Second Copy

Position the text over the copy where you want it to lay (I usually put text at about shoulder height) and then make a copy of the two pieces positioned together.

THREE
Cut Out the Figure

Cut out the shape of the text and the figure.

FOUR
Soften the Text

Soften the text by painting a transparent coat of Titan Buff acrylic paint or another neutral color.

Moment

What other patterns could you use in your collage character's torso? Numbers? Letters? Music or architecture? How could you make yours different?

GLUING WITH GEL MEDIUM

I use Golden's acrylic gel medium as my glue to create collages. You can use it to glue lightweight items such as papers and even small 3-D objects such as dominoes, keys and letter tiles. Just like using any wet glue, there is a trick to gluing your papers down without getting bubbles. Here's what works for me!

ONE
Brush on the Medium

Apply gel medium to your art surface, using a brush that has been dampened with water.

TWO
Add Your Image

Lay the image into the wet medium and then smooth it down from the center pressing outward, using more gel medium over the top. This pushes the bubbles to the edge of the paper and helps to avoid wrinkles.

THREE
Adhere an Object

To apply a 3-D object, brush a generous amount of gel medium onto the back of the item.

FOUR
Clean-Up

Press the piece onto the art surface and clean up any excess gel medium with a brush.

Dressing Your Figures

They say clothes maketh the man. Well, I have to agree. By adding simple "outfits" to your collage people, you can easily create a variety of looks, from silly to formal, and wacky to serious. All it takes are a few simple cuts with your scissors!

PANTS

I like to give my male collage figures big circus-type pants, but you might like a more sophisticated look. By starting with this simple pattern for creating pants, you can then alter it to create a wide variety of fashionable looks. Make pants with big waists, skinny pants, shorts, low rise, high waisted . . . boot-cut, flared pants anyone?

ONE
Measure Waist Width

Lay a piece of paper or fabric over your figure at the spot you want the waist to be. Mark the width with a pencil. I make my pants on the big side because it looks lighthearted and humorous.

TWO
Measure the Length

Decide how long you want the pants to be and mark the spot.

THREE
Cut Out Rectangle

Cut out the rectangle you have just measured.

FOUR
Fold and Cut

Fold the rectangle in half lengthwise and cut out a triangle along the folded edge.

FIVE
Use Scrap as a Hat

Voila! You now have a pair of pants and you can use the triangle as a funny hat!

SKIRT

Could this be any easier? I make skirts mid-calf length to leave room to add legs, but you might prefer a more formal, full-length look. What other kinds of skirts could you come up with? Mini? Knee-length? Hoop skirt?

ONE
Mark the Waist Width

Lay a piece of paper or fabric over your figure at the spot you would like your lady's waistband and mark the desired width with a pencil.

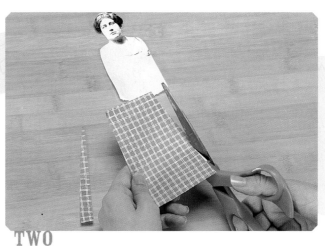

TWO
Trim to an A-Line Shape

Decide on the length of the skirt, and then cut a slight A-line shape from the rectangle.

CREATING TEXTURED BACKGROUNDS

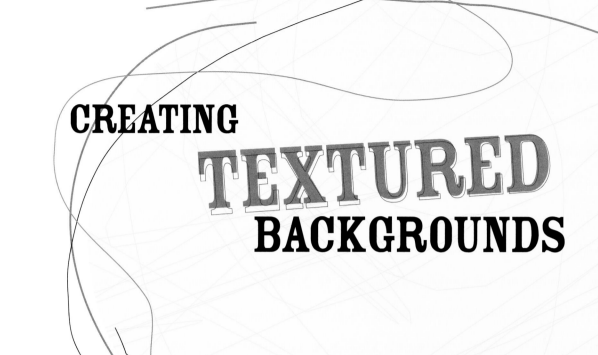

WHEN WORKING IN COLLAGE YOU DON'T NEED TO BUY EXPENSIVE MATERIALS AND SUPPLIES.

You can produce wonderful works of art with items that you may already have around the house. You'll be amazed at the textures and layers you can create!

In this section, I will share eight background techniques that I often experiment with in my own artwork. Each of the backgrounds can be used individually or can be mixed with other background techniques for unlimited results. A few of the surfaces we will create are a crackle-paint effect with Elmer's Glue, an antique surface treatment using masking tape, and a resist with dishwasher rinse aid to create a weathered paint look!

It's important to me to have an interesting background as a starting point for collage. I find that if I have a beautiful and interesting background, the rest of the composition falls into place more easily. I usually start on backgrounds without having a preconceived idea of how the collage will look. I am simply along for the ride, first starting with one color and one technique and then moving to the next. I encourage you to do the same. Don't start with any plans, simply dive in and see what happens!

For the examples in this section I am using a sheet of canvas pad to demonstrate the techniques, but you could use just about any surface—an altered book, journal, stretched canvas, cigar box . . . .

ELMER'S GLUE CRACKLE

Everyone loves the look of crackled paint, but who wants to pay all the money to buy expensive crackling mediums? I know I don't! Did you know you can create amazing crackled paint simply using Elmer's Glue-All? The best part about this technique is that you can use it on furniture or whatever surface you like.

I have experimented with different types of craft glue and found that this works best with Elmer's Glue-All, but you could also try other water-based glues and see if they work too.

What you will need

○ surface (paper canvas) ○ acrylic paint, one or two colors
○ 1-inch (25mm) brush ○ water ○ Elmer's Glue-All

Little Crackle

ONE
Spread the Glue

Drizzle just enough glue onto the paper to have enough to smear around. Using your fingers, spread the glue over the surface until it is just tacky. I like it to be nice and smooth, with no "grains" of glue.

TWO
Paint Over the Glue

Using the brush and a touch of water, apply acrylic paint over the glue. If you keep your strokes in one direction, the crackle will all be in one direction. Try changing directions when painting to see what effects you get. Be careful not to overwork the paint.

THREE
Dry the Paint

Next, take your heat gun and apply heat to the paint and glue surface and watch as crackles appear! (You can also allow it to air dry.)

When drying with a heat gun, make sure not to get too close to your art surface, as it can warp your canvas and make acrylic paint bubble. It is best to hold your gun or hair dryer about 10" (25cm) from your artwork.

TRY THIS!

Big Crackle

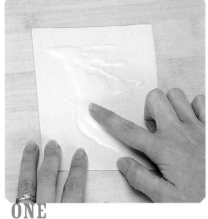

ONE
Spread a Heavy Glue Coat

This time, apply a heavier coat of glue and spread it around (there should be enough glue to equal the amount that you would use when making a peanut butter sandwich).

TWO
Mix Paint Into the Glue

Drop several drops of fluid acrylic paint into the glue and then spread it around with your brush. Don't overwork it; simply use your brush to spread the paint over top of the glue.

THREE
Dry With Heat or Air

Keep your heat gun further away this time, or just let the surface air dry. See how there are much bigger crackles now? You can easily see where I changed direction with my brush, so the cracks changed direction too.

Moment

This method works well over dictionary pages because the cracks actually are big enough to reveal the words underneath.

TOM LIKED HIS PRIZE · · · I painted the cigar box a light blue, then added an Elmer's Glue crackle in the back of the box using Titan Buff. This created a nice crackle, but not one that was so bright that it would distract from the rest of the assemblage. I assembled my piece using various items such as bingo balls and text from an old book. I painted the bingo balls and the sides of the cigar box dark blue so they would tie everything together, yet provide enough contrast with the background. Finally, I used gel medium to glue everything in.

PLASTIC WRAP CRINKLE

This technique is a simple and easy way to get a background with a lot of depth. To me, it often looks like stained glass. I think it is especially effective when used on small areas of a canvas or used as a jump start for a background composition. In the faux finishing world, this method is sometimes called frottage.

What you will need

○ surface (paper canvas) ○ acrylic paint, one or two colors
○ 1-inch (25mm) brush ○ water ○ plastic wrap

TWO
Lay on Plastic

Place a piece of plastic wrap over the paint.

ONE
Paint With One or Two Colors

Squeeze a dab of paint onto your palette and add a bit of water, using your brush. You want your paint to be the consistency of watercolor. Add puddles of color to your surface. If you are using more than one color, mix the two colors together in places.

If your plastic wrap still has wet paint on it after you remove it, try making a print with the plastic wrap on a new piece of paper.

TRY THIS!

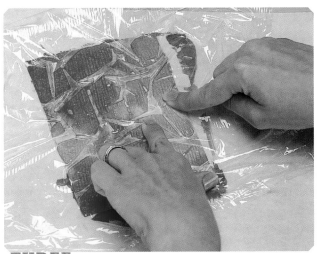

THREE
Set Aside to Dry

Through the plastic wrap, smoosh the paint around with your fingers. Then set the piece aside to dry. (Don't dry using a heat gun because it can melt the plastic wrap.)

FOUR
Remove the Plastic

After the paint has dried completely, gently peel off the plastic wrap to reveal the texture.

Helen picked up the bird.

HELEN PICKED UP THE BIRD ··· After painting the entire cigar box yellow, I glued my main figure to watercolor paper using gel medium and added a little Titan Buff for interest. To create the hills in the background I applied the plastic wrap technique to a sheet of canvas pad using a few shades of green. After it was dry, I cut the finished piece into a rolling-hill shape and glued it to the back of the cigar box. I secured the rest of the elements using gel medium and as a finishing touch, I painted the sides of the cigar box red.

LAYERED MASKING TAPE

Remember making masking tape lampshades in Girl Scouts? Well, I am still using a variation on that technique! By using masking tape you can create a layered and distressed look for your background. It's easy, inexpensive and fun! What could be better?

What you will need

○ surface (paper canvas) ○ masking tape in several widths
○ gel medium ○ heat gun (optional) ○ acrylic paint, in three colors
○ 1-inch brush ○ paper towel

ONE
Apply Layers of Tape

Tear and apply several pieces of masking tape to the surface, varying direction and size. Continue until the surface is covered. I like to tear some of the pieces along the long sides. Burnish all the pieces down well with a bone folder or the handle of your scissors.

TWO
Add Gel Medium, Let Dry

Trim off the excess pieces or fold them under. Use gel medium over the top to ensure the piece will be archival. Blow dry with a heat gun, or set aside to dry.

THREE
Paint Over the Tape

Begin adding color to your surface, using acrylic paint over the tape. Mix the colors as you go.

FOUR
Buff Off the Paint

Work in the paint and buff it with a paper towel. This will reveal the texture, but also remove some of the paint. Some places I will leave less paint and some I will leave more.

FIVE
Repeat With More Paint

Go back and add some more paint with your fingers along the edges, and buff it again in the same way.

SHE NOTICED THE DRESS · · · I began this piece by securing strips of masking tape to the canvas. After sealing it with a layer of gel medium, I painted the tape pink. I glued the figure down to the canvas using gel medium and then I added the finishing touches with an ink pen.

SKETCHING INTO WET PAINT

Next time you are in a gallery, look closely at the surface of various paintings. Sometimes you can see where an artist had sketched out ideas, or scratched away at layers of paint. I love to see this in artworks because it lends a sense of history to the piece. You can imagine all the stages of evolution that it went through until the artist was satisfied. It's easy to achieve a similar feel to your artwork. Try drawing and sketching out rough ideas into wet acrylic paint. It will leave a hint of texture and a layered look to your artwork.

What you will need

○ surface (paper canvas) ○ heavy-bodied acrylic paint ○ paint brush
○ pencil ○ paper towel

ONE
Paint Your Surface

Spread paint over the surface. Here, I am using white paint but you could use any color as long as it is heavy-bodied or a thick, tube-type of paint.

TWO
Sketch With a Pencil

Using a pencil, draw shapes and plot out your composition into the paint. Let everything dry.

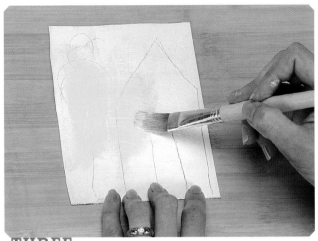

THREE
Paint Over the Sketch

Paint a second color over the dried image.

FOUR
Remove Excess Paint

With a paper towel, dab over the wet paint, removing most of it. See how the paint settles into the drawn areas?

GOOD FRIENDS DON'T CARE WHAT YOU WEAR ··· I painted the entire canvas a dark orange. When it was dry, I painted over it with white and then sketched into the white paint while it was still wet, using a pencil. I marked lines and swirls in the upper right portion of the canvas and along the bottom.

Technique 5

TISSUE PAPER LAYER

Using gift-wrapping tissue to add texture in your artwork is an easy way to create a distressed and complex-looking background. When I come home from the art store with a stack of new canvases, usually I'll break them in with a layer of tissue paper texture. It is simple and inexpensive!

What you will need

○ surface (paper canvas) ○ acrylic paint, in two colors
○ 1-inch (25mm) brush ○ white gift tissue ○ heat gun
(optional) ○ paper towel

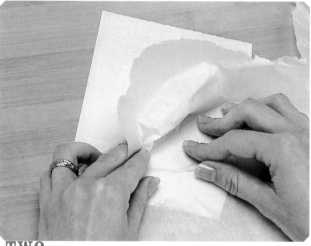

TWO
Add Some Tissue Paper

Tear off a piece of tissue that covers the majority of the surface.

ONE
Paint Your Surface

Apply a layer of acrylic paint to the surface. Here, I used Titan Buff.

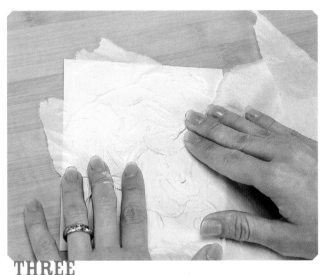

THREE
Create a Pleasing Pattern

Smoosh the tissue around until you have a pattern you like. I like the tissue to be heavier in some spots and lighter or altogether missing in others.

FOUR
Add a Second Color

Let the tissue and paint dry completely before moving on. You can use a heat gun if you are feeling impatient. Now using the brush, begin applying a new color over the entire surface.

FIVE
Blot Off Excess Paint

Blot excess wet paint off of the surface with a paper towel.

THEY MIGHT DISAPPROVE OF YOU AND WHAT YOU DO · · · After painting this piece a light green, I layered white tissue paper into the wet paint and added cream and white paint on top. I also added bits of dress pattern tissue, creating the arrow that points at the man's head and the hill along the bottom.

RINSE AID RESIST

You can use dishwasher rinse aid as a resist to create a peeling and aged paint look. This technique looks wonderful when done over collaged papers or over a contrasting color of paint. If you are doing it over a collaged background, I recommend sealing the papers with gel medium before starting.

What you will need

○ surface (paper canvas) ○ gel medium (optional) ○ acrylic paint, in two colors ○ 1-inch (25mm) brush ○ water ○ dishwasher rinse aid ○ heat gun (optional) ○ paper towel

TWO
Drop Rinse Aid Into the Paint

Hold your surface up, and drop the rinse aid into the wet paint. Let it run down through the paint to create a streaky look.

ONE
Add Thinned Paint to Your Surface

Apply a layer of watery paint to the surface.

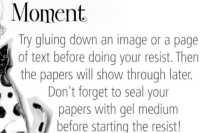

Moment

Try gluing down an image or a page of text before doing your resist. Then the papers will show through later. Don't forget to seal your papers with gel medium before starting the resist!

THREE
Remove Dried Paint

Let this layer dry, either with a heat gun or air dry. Take a damp paper towel and rub it across the surface to remove excess paint. See how the surface resisted paint where the rinse aid ran?

FOUR
Try Adding a Second Color

After the paint has dried, it's fun to go back and add a second color. Reapply a second watery layer of acrylic paint. Here I used a reddish color, and added more rinse aid into the wet paint.

FIVE
Remove Dried Paint

Just like with the first color, remove the excess paint with a damp paper towel.

EDNA LOVED HER DOG VERY MUCH
···I created a first resist using the dishwashing rinse and a light blue. After that was dry I did another resist on top using a light green mixed with cream to give the background more depth. Here I chose to layer the resist technique twice but you could layer it as many times as you would like; each time you add another layer it will create more depth.

CONTACT PAPER SHAPES

I like to use contact paper shapes to create a "reverse mask" of sorts. By lightly adhering to my shapes, the paint will seep underneath and will create a look that has depth and interest. You can use punches to make your contact paper shapes or you can cut them freehand. I do a mix of both, depending on the look I want.

What you will need

○ surface (paper canvas) ○ contact paper ○ decorative punches
○ acrylic paint ○ 1-inch (25mm) brush ○ water ○ paper towels

ONE
Cut Out Shapes

Cut out shapes from the contact paper with either scissors or a decorative punch.

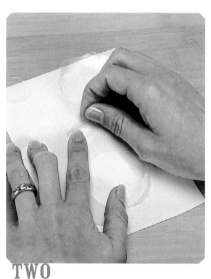

TWO
Stick Shapes to Surface

Stick the shapes lightly to the paper canvas. Don't burnish down the contact paper.

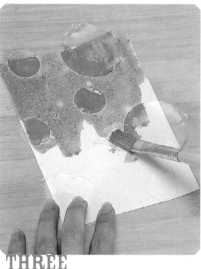

THREE
Apply Paint Over the Shapes

Apply a thin layer of watery paint over the entire surface including the shapes.

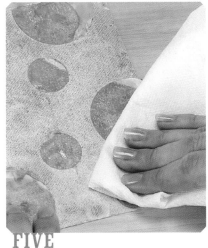

FOUR
Let Paint Seep Under Shapes

The paint will seep under the contact paper shapes, creating a soft edge. Encourage this further by moving the paint around with your fingers on top of the plastic shape to work the paint in.

FIVE
Blot Paint Around the Shapes

Use paper towels to blot over the shapes to create darker images.

SIX
Remove the Contact Paper

Let the paint dry, then gently remove the contact paper shapes.

NIGHT OF THE ORANGE FLOWERS ··· I began this piece by cutting flower shapes out of contact paper. I placed them onto the canvas lightly and then painted the entire canvas with a light orange. After the paint was dry I lifted the contact paper flowers off and darker orange flowers were left behind. I finished the collage using an image of a little girl, blue stars and ink pen line drawing.

If you are using a punch to cut your contact paper shapes, try sliding in an extra piece of scrap paper on top of your contact paper and then punching. This helps the punch work more smoothly.

TRY THIS!

USING BACKGROUND TEXTURES TOGETHER

NEXT, WE'LL EXPLORE MIXING AND MATCHING THE TECHNIQUES FROM THE LAST SECTION.

All of these techniques can be mixed to create unlimited results. You could do the tissue paper technique and then do the crackle technique on top of that, or you could start with plastic wrap and later add masking tape texture . . . the possibilities are truly endless.

As I create each of the artwork in this section, I'll let you know what I am thinking as I move along: how one item leads to the next item and one idea to the next idea. I'll be working on a cigar box, an altered book and on canvas. But you could do these techniques on just about any surface from a mint tin to a mini-shrine.

I encourage you to pursue your own path for your collages. Try not to worry about making mistakes. Remember that you can always layer another piece of paper on top or cover over with paint. Also, don't forget layering adds the sense of history to our collages that we love so much. So let's jump in and see what we can create!

What you will need

○ balsa wood cigar box ○ craft knife
○ sandpaper ○ gesso ○ 1-inch
(25mm) brush ○ contact paper
○ scissors and/or decorative punches
○ acrylic paints (four colors and
Titan Buff) ○ paper towel ○ pencil
○ dishwasher rinse aid ○ copy
images and collage items ○ gel
medium ○ fabric scraps ○ watercolor paper ○ canvas pad ○ gift
tissue ○ Elmer's Glue-All ○ fine
point pen ○ small wooden spools

TEXTURAL TECHNIQUES

ELMER'S GLUE CRACKLE (PAGE 20)
...
SKETCHING INTO WET PAINT (PAGE 26)
...
TISSUE PAPER LAYER (PAGE 28)
...
RINSE AID RESIST (PAGE 30)
...
CONTACT PAPER SHAPES (PAGE 32)

Starry Night
(CIGAR BOX)

This first collage exercise gives you a chance to practice contact paper shapes, tissue paper, rinse aid resist, drawing in paint, and Elmer's Glue crackle techniques. Notice how each layer of paint adds more depth and interest? I'll be using a cigar box for this project but you could do the same techniques in an altered book, in a journal, on a canvas or on just about any surface you like.

Working in a cigar box is a wonderful format to create a 3-D collage or assemblage. Cigar boxes come in many sizes: square, rectangle, cube, etc. Some boxes are created using wonderful woods with inlay and lovely designs. The cigar boxes that I like to use are made from inexpensive balsa wood and are covered in paper. It's easy to remove the lid from this type of box and use it in a shadow-box format.

Experiment by cutting different shapes from your contact paper, both with various punches and freehand. The sky's the limit!

TRY THIS!

ONE
Remove Lid

Remove the lid from the cigar box, using a craft knife.

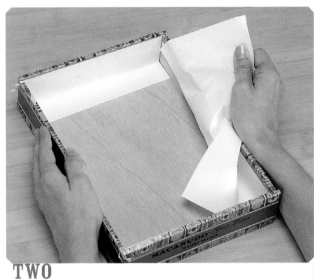

TWO
Remove Labels

Remove all of the paper lining and as much of the labels as possible.

THREE
Sand Rough Spots

Lightly sand over all of the remaining paper areas to even out the surface.

FOUR
Apply Gesso to the Box

Apply gesso to both the inside and the outside of the box, using a paintbrush.

FIVE
Cut Out Contact Stars

Let the gesso dry completely. Cut out several star shapes from contact paper. I wanted these stars to be irregular in shape, so I cut them out freehand.

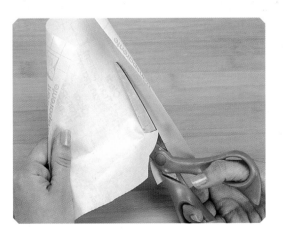

SIX
Paint Over Stars

Stick the stars into the back of the box, in an arrangement that you find pleasing. Then add a watery layer of acrylic paint with your paintbrush and completely cover the stars. Here I used a light sage green color.

SEVEN
Blot Excess Paint

Add the paint to the entire inside of the box, and blot all of the excess paint up with a paper towel.

EIGHT
Outline With Pencil

Allow your paint to air dry and then peel up the contact star shapes. I thought it might look nice to add a little extra definition, so I outlined my star shapes with a pencil.

NINE
Apply New Paint and Rinse Aid

Apply your second color to the back of the box, then drip the rinse aid at one end, and let it run through the paint. I felt like I wanted to add a little more depth to my background so I added the rinse aid resist on top. See how the addition of another technique adds more interest?

TEN
Experiment With Figure Options

Dry thoroughly and then remove the excess color with a damp paper towel. Find a collage image that you like and that you think looks good against the created background. (I like to try several options before deciding.) Hold each item up to your background and see how you feel about it. Often I have a gut reaction when I know one is right. If you're not sure, let one item sit on your background and come back to it later.

ELEVEN
Choose Fabric for Clothes

After deciding on an image, choose a fabric that will work well for clothing. I think this orange fabric looks great with the green background and will make a splendid skirt.

TWELVE
Mount Figure

Tear out the rough image of a skirt and adhere the image and the fabric to a piece of watercolor paper using gel medium. When working in 3-D, I like to build my figure on a sturdy piece of watercolor paper so that I can layer it in later.

THIRTEEN
Cut Out the Image

Apply a second coat of gel medium over the entire image and fabric. I wanted to tone down the starkness of the white paper that the text is copied on, so I added a wash of Titan Buff acrylic paint. Cut out the entire image.

FOURTEEN
Create a Crackled House

Next, create some Elmer's glue crackle on a separate piece of canvas pad paper, using a color that complements the background. After it is dry, cut out the shape of a house.

FIFTEEN
Add Tissue Texture

Set the house and the figure aside. Glue in a strip of tissue to the back of the cigar box to create a horizon line. Stain the tissue with thinned acrylic. I often like to add a horizon line to my compositions because I feel it helps "ground" the composition.

SIXTEEN
Soften Stars

After I held my figure in the cigar box to test her placement, I decided that the stars behind her head might be too distracting. If yours are too, add a little bit more acrylic paint in the same color on top of the stars to tone them down.

SEVENTEEN
Create Legs and Shoes

Set a piece of watercolor paper under the figure's skirt and draw on some legs and shoes. If you are unsure about free-handing your own shoes, try tracing them from a clip art image.

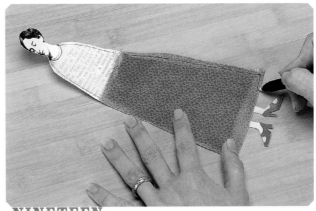

EIGHTEEN
Color in Elements

Add a touch of Titan Buff acrylic paint to the legs and paint the shoes orange (or whatever color matches your skirt.) I decided to give my figure a cute pair of Mary Janes.

NINETEEN
Outline Details

Cut out the legs and shoes, and glue them on with gel medium to the underside of the dress. Loosely outline the figure with a fine point pen.

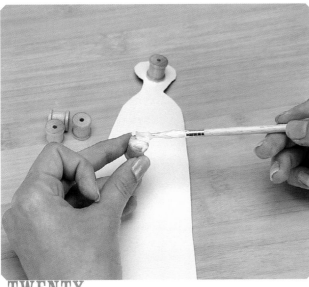

TWENTY
Add Spools to the Back

Using gel medium, adhere several small wooden spools or cubes to the back of the figure. These will create a little lift to the figure and add dimension.

TWENTY-ONE
Add Figure and House

Glue the figure and spools to the back of the cigar box using gel medium. Add the house in the background. I decided my house needed a little extra line work so I added some with a fine point pen. To finish, paint the outside of the box to coordinate.

What if you gave your figure different shoes? How would boots, sneakers, or even bare feet change the feel of the piece? What if you gave her a different skirt? Longer or shorter? Or what if you had two people in the composition instead of one? Would you have combined different techniques together or used different colors?

WHAT IF...

Boating Trip
(ALTERED BOOK)

An altered book can be a journal with blank pages, a children's book or a steamy romance novel.

Look for old books at flea markets, antique stores, used book stores or libraries. The idea is that you can take any book and turn it into art. You can use any of the techniques that I have demonstrated (as well as any additional techniques you can think of) to create an altered book. I would advise covering the pages with a coat of gesso before working on them to make each one more durable and ready to collage on. Then treat the book as your canvas and begin creating!

This collage exercise gives you an opportunity to practice plastic wrap crinkle, tissue paper layer and sketching in paint together. I'll be using an altered book as my surface for this project but you could do the same techniques in a cigar box, journal, on canvas or just about any surface you like.

TEXTURAL TECHNIQUES

PLASTIC WRAP CRINKLE (PAGE 22)
...
SKETCHING INTO WET PAINT (PAGE 26)
...
TISSUE PAPER LAYER (PAGE 28)

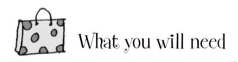 What you will need

○ old thrift store book ○ gesso or gel medium ○ 1-inch (25mm) brush ○ tissue paper ○ acrylic paint (Titan Buff, and additional colors) ○ pencil ○ paper towel ○ water ○ plastic wrap ○ copy images ○ colored paper ○ scissors ○ fine point pen ○ markers (optional)

ONE
Choose a Book

Choose a book with a size and weight that you like and are comfortable with.

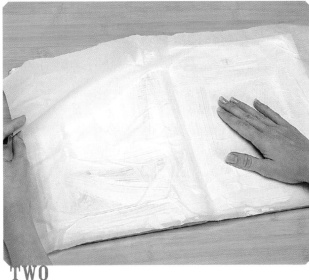

TWO
Apply Gesso and Tissue

Open the book to a place where you would like to start working. Coat the pages with gesso or gel medium to prime. Add a sheet of tissue paper into the wet gesso and smooth it down a bit, but not completely; a few wrinkles are good!

THREE
Sketch in Composition

Brush additional gesso or white paint over the tissue, and then map out your rough composition with a pencil in the wet paint. Here I am thinking that I might like my piece to have an ocean of water at the bottom and maybe a person in a boat. I mapped it out in rough pencil lines, into the wet paint, to test my idea.

FOUR
Apply Paint and Blot Excess

Let everything dry and then trim off the excess tissue. Brush on yellow paint loosely over both of the pages and then blot off the excess with a paper towel.

FIVE
Create Plastic Wrap Water Section

Brush on a watery layer of blue acrylic paint in the lower third of the book, following the pencil line you made earlier. Lay plastic wrap onto the wet paint, then smoosh it around to create interesting shapes.

SIX
Choose Figure for the Boat

After the paint has dried and you have removed the plastic wrap, add a wash of the same blue acrylic paint over the dried texture. This softens the texture a little bit. (I felt mine was too busy.) Cut a simple boat shape from colored paper and set the boat on top of the water. Choose one or two figures from your collection and decide who looks best in the boat. Try several options. First I thought I wanted two people in my boat, but then I decided I preferred one solitary grumpy looking man instead. I liked the humor of the grouchy man in the happy, polka-dotted boat.

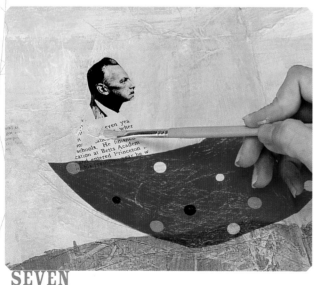

SEVEN
Place Boat Over Figure

Use your brush and gel medium to adhere the figure to the page. Add the boat on top of the figure and tone down the white text on the figure, using Titan Buff acrylic paint.

EIGHT
Add Clouds

Loosely paint in fluffy clouds in the sky portion of the pages.

NINE
Sketch Out More Elements

Practice adding other elements into your composition by sketching them on scrap pieces of paper. I felt that my man seemed a little lonely all by himself and maybe he needed another element. I placed a fish, drawn on a scrap of paper, on the page and decided it was just what he needed.

TEN
Add Final Elements in Pen

Once you have a composition you like, begin drawing in the individual elements with a fine tip pen.

ELEVEN
Color in With Marker

Color in some of the elements with paint or marker. I decided my fish needed a little color. I chose orange because it is close enough to red to add another warm element to the composition without repeating the red, and it did the trick.

Moment

Feeling stuck? Try experimenting with background techniques until you are inspired. Simply by working with the materials, you'll be coaxing your creative side to come out and play and soon you'll be on a roll.

What if you gave your composition a different boat? What about a sail added to the boat? A yacht? A tugboat? Could you have used another technique or different colors? What if you filled the boat with people? What if the man had a funny hat? How would all these different elements change the mood of the piece? What else could the man have been fishing for?

WHAT IF...

Kate was just being childish

What you will need

○ contact paper ○ decorative circle punches ○ 9" × 12" (23cm × 30cm) canvas ○ acrylic paints ○ 1-inch (25mm) brush ○ water ○ paper towels ○ dishwasher rinse aid ○ spray bottle ○ masking tape, various widths ○ gel medium ○ collage images ○ fabric scraps ○ red masking tape ○ pencil ○ fine point pen ○ marker (optional) ○ ribbon

TEXTURAL TECHNIQUES

LAYERED MASKING TAPE (24)

•••

RINSE AID RESIST (30)

•••

CONTACT PAPER SHAPES (32)

Childish Kate
(CANVAS)

The couple in this collage appear as if they might be out on a date. The text along the bottom suggests they had a little spat. What could Kate have been pouting about? I wonder! I enjoy the air of humor and the partially told story in this piece. It's important to note that this artwork could have turned out very differently if I had used another strip of text or combined different collage images from my stash. So jump into this exercise with whatever images you happen to have on hand and see where your story leads you.

We'll be combining contact paper shapes, layered masking tape, and rinse aid resist techniques. I'll be using a canvas for this project but you could do the same techniques in an altered book, journal, cigar box or whichever surface you prefer.

Collect sayings from romance novels and other books, cut them out with a craft knife and keep them in a candy mint tin or other container. That way they will be ready when you need them.

TRY THIS!

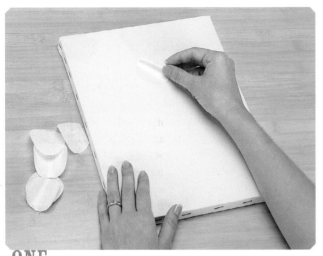

ONE
Punch Out Circles

Punch out your circle shapes from the contact paper. A total of four or five is good. Lightly apply your shapes to the canvas. Here I'm not sure what my background will end up looking like, but I love polka dots so it seems as good a place as any to start.

TWO
Work Paint Under Shapes

Add a thin, watery layer of paint to your canvas, covering the circle shapes and spreading paint under the contact paper with your brush. Blot over the paint with paper towels to remove excess paint around the shapes. Try to leave a little heavier paint in some areas than in others to add interest. I decided to use blue paint but you could use any color. Try mixing two colors together and allow them to blend under the contact paper.

THREE
Add Paint and Rinse Aid

Let the canvas dry completely before moving on. Remove the contact paper and let the paint that was under the shapes dry a little more if it is still wet. Brush a watery mix of paint over the entire canvas and then spray dishwashing rinse aid into the wet paint, using a spray bottle. I liked the direction my piece was taking with the polka dots, but it needed more oomph. The rinse aid resist did the trick and added more depth to the background.

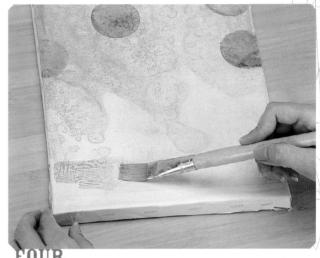

FOUR
Apply and Stain Tape

Let the canvas dry and, using a damp paper towel, remove the soapy residue. Add rows of masking tape to the lower half of the canvas. Don't forget to adhere the tape with gel medium if you want to ensure longevity. Dry the gel medium and then stain the tape with paint. I often like to have some sort of horizon line element. Here I thought I could use the masking tape to create a subtle horizon line in the background.

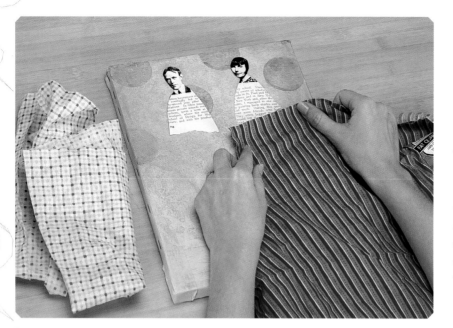

FIVE
Pick Out Fabric

Choose one or two figures from your collection that you feel belong with your background. Then choose some fabric for your figures to wear. I felt that my background was finished and ready for a focal point on top. I sorted through my collage elements, holding up different figures against my background until I found a couple that clicked. I liked the way this couple seemed as if they had a conversation that recently ended.

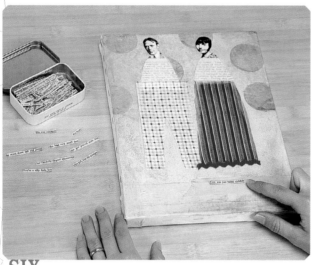

SIX
Play With Some Text

Cut out clothes from the fabric and, using gel medium, adhere the figure heads and their clothes to the canvas (I added a piece of rickrack to the bottom of the lady's skirt, too). After the figures are glued down, choose lines of text from your stash that create a story for the figures. I chose the phrase "Kate was just being childish" but what if I had chosen "nice girl, but she gossips" or "he stood there tall and proud"? It's fun to experiment with sayings, because each one gives the piece a different feel.

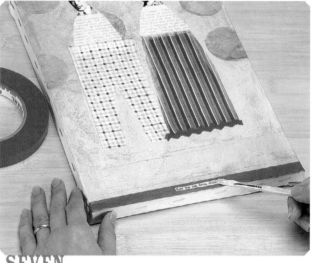

SEVEN
Add Tape and Text

I felt that my collage still needed more weight at the bottom to ground it. I decided to use a line of colored tape as a foundation for my chosen text. Masking tape comes in many colors; choose one that suits your piece. Add your line of text, using gel medium, on top of the tape.

Don't be afraid to draw on your own collages. We want to see it! It will make your work more real, and uniquely yours. No one else can draw the way that you can—embrace it!

TRY THIS!

48

EIGHT
Add Body Parts

Sketch out the body parts for your figures in pencil, and then go over them with a fine point black pen. Worried about drawing hands and feet? Leave them off or draw stick feet (it'll make it even more quirky). Or you can practice drawing your body parts on a separate piece of paper until you feel comfortable.

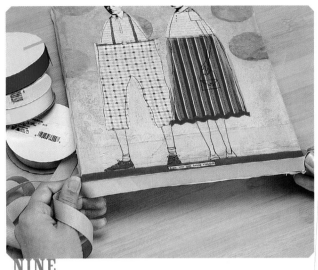

NINE
Try on Different Colors

With paint or marker, color in the suspenders and shoes and wherever else you wish to add color. I decided to give my man red suspenders and shoes to repeat the red from Kate's dress. One way to finish off your canvas is to wrap ribbon around the outside. Try different colors to see which sets your piece off the best. Here, I thought the blue was a little too subtle, so I decided on red for more punch.

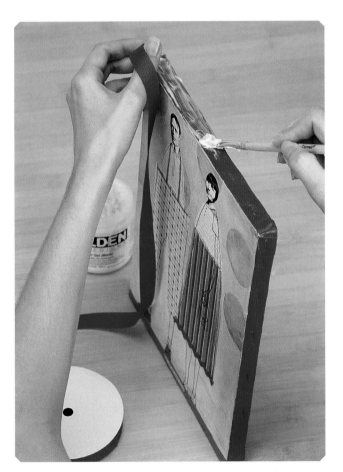

TEN
Finish Off With Ribbon

If your chosen ribbon is just a fraction too narrow for the depth of the canvas, you can paint the sides to match the ribbon. Then if the canvas shows through, it won't be noticed. Cut a length of ribbon to go all the way around the canvas and glue it to the sides with gel medium.

What if this collage was done in a cigar box? How would the extra dimension change the feel? What if the people had more accessories or hats? Different shoes? How would a different text element on the artwork change the mood of the collage? What if there was patterned ribbon around the edge?

WHAT IF…

USING PRINTMAKING IN COLLAGE

XEROGRAPHIC PRINTMAKING IS ALSO KNOWN AS PAPER PLATE LITHOGRAPHY.

This is because it uses the same techniques that are used in lithographic printmaking, but instead of using a big heavy stone as our plate, we use a paper Xerox copy or photocopy.

I learned this technique at the Corcoran College of Art + Design from my printmaking teacher, Georgia Deal. In college we used large printmaking presses to transfer our prints. After I graduated I wanted to continue using this technique but didn't have thousands of dollars for an expensive press. Through trial and error, I discovered that you could get wonderful prints using a metal spoon and rubbing. I also wanted to find a way to get crisper prints, like the kinds we made with the presses in the printmaking studio. After experimenting, I found that I could use a pasta machine. Although the width of the pasta machine sets a limitation on size, it provides a cheap and easy way to achieve good quality prints.

Some people find they prefer the spoon method, some the pasta machine. I'll show you both so you can decide for yourself. It's a lot of fun to try, and with a little practice you'll be a pro!

PRINTING WITH ONE COLOR

For our first step in printmaking, I thought we'd try creating a print using one color on watercolor paper, using the spoon method. Before we begin, check that you are using regular laser copies and not inkjet prints. You might want to make a few extra copies of your image so if it doesn't work for you the first time you can try again. After a little practice you'll have the steps down and you'll be ready to move on to a more complicated print, but for now, let's start simple!

What you will need

○ photocopy ○ gum arabic ○ waxed paper ○ spray bottle with water
○ damp sponge ○ palette paper ○ oil paint ○ linseed oil ○ brayer
watercolor paper ○ spoon

Spoon

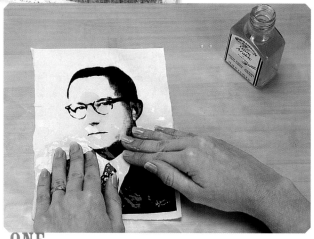

ONE
Work in Gum Arabic

Tear around the copy image. Working on a piece of waxed paper, apply gum arabic to the back side and rub around just enough to get it wet. Then flip your copy over and apply gum arabic to the front side. This will allow the gum arabic on the back to soak in as you work the front. Be liberal with the gum arabic. You want enough so it covers all of the paper, but not so much that you have a giant puddle that takes forever to dry.

TWO
Massage the Paper

Massage the medium into every area of the paper. Work it until it almost feels dry and is no longer goopy-feeling or sticky. This could take a couple of minutes so be patient. Rub gently or you could tear the paper. You might be able to see in this example that the gum has fully soaked in and has even made a few water-marks or blotches on the copy. That is good. It means the gum arabic is soaking in.

THREE
Dampen the Image

Spray your copy lightly with a spritz of water, then dampen a sponge and gently wipe it over the image. This step will remove the excess gum arabic from the toner areas of the copy. Be careful not to scrub the paper. It's better to err on the side of caution with less wiping than too much.

FOUR
Add Linseed Oil to Paint

Squeeze out a bit of oil paint onto your paper palette and add just a tiny drop of linseed oil. If your paint is very dry or clumpy, you might need to add a little more linseed oil. Your oil paint should be smooth and spread easily with your brayer.

FIVE
Ink Up the Brayer

Work the paint and the oil together with your brayer. Try not to mash the brayer into the paint. Let the brayer do the work and rub it gently through the paint and oil. I recommend brayering through the paint about 5-8 times in different directions to get a nice even spread of paint on the brayer. See how the paint has a suede-like texture? That is the texture your paint should be.

SIX
Apply Ink to the Image

Bray your ink onto the prepped image. You should still be able to lightly see the copy. Don't put on so much ink that it completely obscures the image.

PRINTING PRIMER

A good Xerox plate (or copy) will ensure a good print. Color copies and inkjet copies will not work for this process! I have had the best luck using second generation black and white toner copies to achieve the best contrast of whites and darks. Remember that shades of gray tend to blend and become a solid color.

Moment

"Why couldn't I use block printing ink?" You can! I simply use oil paints because they work just as well, come in a larger variety of colors and are easier to find than printing inks.

SEVEN
Rinse Off the Paper

Using your spray bottle, spray the image, holding it over a plate or bowl to catch the runoff. Continue spraying until all the oil paint is released from the white areas of the paper. If your paint is not releasing it could be because you didn't rub in the gum arabic correctly. It's the gum arabic that allows the paint to release from the white areas. This is the time to make sure everything is cleaned up and there is nothing on the paper that you don't want on your finished print. Continue spraying until all stray bits of oil paint are removed.

EIGHT
Lay Copy Onto Surface

Place the inked copy face down onto your receiving surface. Here I am using watercolor paper. It's good to have your copy wet and drippy when you place it onto the paper.

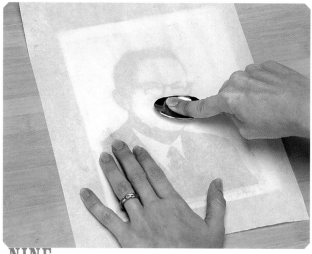

NINE
Burnish With a Spoon

Make sure your copy is flat with no wrinkles. Set a piece of palette paper (matte side up) over the back of the copy and begin working the spoon over the image, pressing firmly in all directions.

TEN
Marvel at Your Work

Ta dah! The image has transferred to the paper beautifully!

A sink with a sprayer makes life much easier on your hands than using a spray bottle. Put paper towels or a plastic plate in the bottom of your sink to catch the oil paint that slides off. Then when you are done, throw the paper towels away.

TRY THIS!

54

PRINTING WITH TWO COLORS

Now that you've tried printing in one color, let's try something a little more involved. Printmaking on fabric is wonderful because it doesn't change the hand of the fabric. It still remains soft. This is a great technique for fiber artists and for artists in general.

What you will need

○ photocopy ○ fabric (muslin works well) ○ gum arabic ○ spray bottle with water ○ damp sponge ○ palette paper ○ oil paints ○ linseed oil ○ brayers (2) ○ waxed paper ○ pasta machine ○ colored pencils

Pasta Machine

ONE
Apply Inks to Image

Tear your copy and your fabric (or other receiving surface) down to a size that is narrow enough to fit through the pasta machine. Apply gum arabic to your image like you did in steps 1–3 on pages 52–53. Prepare two colors of oil paint with linseed oil as you did previously and ink up areas of your copy with the desired color. Here I am using red for the tree and bird, and brown for the face and figure of the girl. I used one brayer for each color, but you could clean off your brayer between colors.

TWO
Place Image Face Down

Rinse off the ink like you did in step 7 on page 54 and then place the copy face down on your trimmed piece of fabric.

THREE
Create a Jacket

Make a jacket for the copy and the fabric by folding a piece of waxed paper around both layers. This will protect your print when you run it through the pasta machine.

Moment

Try scratching into the paint with a toothpick and then printing—the marks that you made will print also. Place a leaf or other element onto your waxed paper after you ink it and then run it through the pasta machine. The leaf will print!

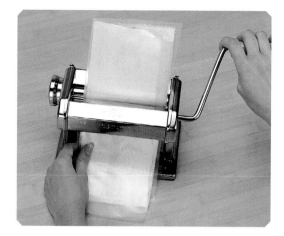

FOUR
Run Print Through Machine

Run the piece through the pasta machine. I use the tightest setting, which on my machine is number 9 on the dial, but each machine is different.

FIVE
Touch Up With Pencil

If an image doesn't come through with as much color or detail as you want, don't worry! You can touch it up with colored pencil. I added a wash of yellow paint around my figure to separate her from the background. Do you have any finishing touches you'd like to make to your print?

XEROGRAPHY CHECKLIST

- Make sure to rub gum arabic on the front and back of the copy until it has soaked in and feels dry, not sticky or soupy.

- If you see wet spots or watermarks on your copy when you are rubbing in the gum arabic that means that it is soaking in well to your copy paper.

- Your ink should be a "suede-like" consistency. If it feels too thick or doesn't slide off your copy paper well when you spray it with water, add a drop of linseed oil to the ink for the next time.

- Allow your copy to remain wet and drippy when you apply it to your receiving surface. You might feel like it should be dry, but it is actually better if it is wet.

- If your ink doesn't slide off your copy easily when you spray it with water, it could be that you need to allow more gum arabic to soak in next time, or you might need to add more linseed oil to your oil paint.

If your pasta machine isn't making the prints dark enough, run a piece of cardstock through with the image to make it bulkier.

TRY THIS!

LAYERING MULTIPLE PRINTS

In this printmaking exercise we'll combine two copies at the same time to create a print. The first copy masks the second, creating layers. The best part is that it looks complicated, but it is very easy to do!

What you will need

○ photocopy ○ watercolor paper ○ waxed paper ○ gum arabic
○ spray bottle with water ○ sponge ○ palette paper ○ oil paints
○ linseed oil ○ brayers (2) ○ spoon or pasta machine

ONE
Trim Copies

Cut your images and watercolor paper so everything will fit in the pasta machine. Here, I am trimming to separate my figure from the background.

TWO
Ink Up Images Separately

Apply gum arabic to the copies as you did previously, and wipe them down with a sponge and water. Ink up one image with one color and the other image with another color. I wanted to use blue for the text image and brown for the figure.

TRY THIS!

If you have words in your copy and you want them to read correctly, set your copying machine to "mirror image" when you are making your copies. That way when you print from the copy, the text will read the right way.

57

THREE
Set Stickers On Image

Rinse off the ink with your spray bottle and then apply dots of paper or stickers down the front of the figure to create "buttons." These dots will act as a mask and not allow the ink to print where I placed them. What else could you use as a mask? A heart shape? Stars?

FOUR
Layer From Front to Back

Place the image of the figure face down onto the watercolor paper. Then place the text page face down on top of the figure.

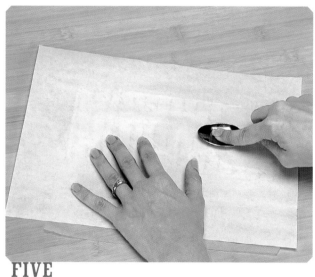

FIVE
Print With Spoon or Pasta Machine

Place the layered papers in a waxed paper jacket and run through the pasta machine, or place a sheet of palette paper, matte side up, on top of the inked images and rub with a spoon.

SIX
Reveal Print

Peel off the copies to reveal the layered print. Use colored pencil if your print needs a little touch up.

CLEAN UP

It is relatively easy to clean your tools when you are finished printing. If you use the disposable paper palette and wax papers for your paints, simply throw them away when you have finished your printing session. To clean your brayer, run it over a dry paper towel to remove excess paint, then wash with grease-cutting, soapy water and wipe with a paper towel. Running a baby wipe through your pasta machine is an easy way to clean it and remove excess gum arabic and inks that might have oozed onto the rollers.

CHINE COLLÉ

Chine Collé was developed by nineteenth-century printers as a way to use thin Chinese and Japanese papers without employing Asian mounting techniques. The term comes from the French, *chine* for Chinese and *collé* for glue. Chine collé is a collage technique used in printmaking whereby a thin piece of collage paper (or fabric) is adhered to a heavier sheet and then they are run through the printing press together.

Why would you use Chine collé rather than just gluing your papers on? Good question! By running the papers through the press, it marries both surfaces together and creates a very smooth edge—making it almost impossible to feel where either paper begins and ends. It's ideal for those who like very smooth papers with no wrinkles or bubbles.

What you will need

○ xerographic print ○ fabric or paper scraps ○ gel medium ○ 1-inch (25mm) brush ○ waxed paper ○ pasta machine ○ fine point pen

ONE
Adhere Pieces to Print

Cut out the pieces you wish to collé onto your printed piece. Apply a thin layer of gel medium to the back. Gently place your items onto the print. Here, I am using fabric but you could use tissue papers or other papers as well.

TWO
Run Image Through Machine

Place the image in a waxed paper jacket and run it through the pasta machine.

THREE
Add Detail With a Pen

Add fun details with a fine point pen. Here I gave the girl's party hat a tie-on string, and I lightly outlined the heart and hat.

CREATIVELY COMBINING PAPER & FABRIC

IN THIS CHAPTER, WE'LL EXPLORE USING WATER-SOLUBLE OIL PASTELS IN COMBINATION WITH UNSTRETCHED CANVAS TO CREATE CUSTOM-COLORED FABRIC.

Working on unstretched canvas will add a new twist to your collages. The frayed edges and rough texture make even new artworks look "found," like remnants of another place and time.

I'll show you how to make an unusual book on canvas that solves the problem of how to display your lightweight handmade books when you've finished them. We'll make a 3-D assemblage incorporating a handmade doll and printing onto Plexiglas. We'll also create a fun and funky wall hanging that will add pizzazz to any room.

COLOR-STAINING UNPRIMED FABRIC

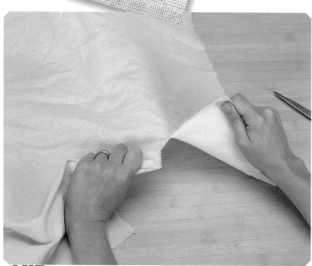

Staining your unprimed canvas or fabric is easy. In this section you'll find simple steps that you can use to prepare your canvas for any of the following projects. Using water-soluble oil pastels and gel medium, you can stain your canvas so that it is any color you want. This creates a soft look that can't be achieved using printed fabrics.

What you will need

○ unprimed duck canvas (or fabric) ○ scissors ○ gel medium ○ water
○ 1-inch (25mm) brush ○ water-soluble oil pastels ○ acrylic paint

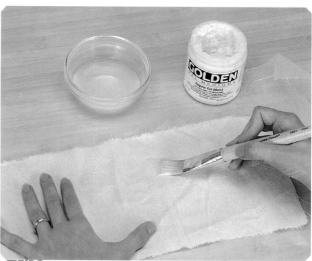

TWO
Coat One Side

Cover one side of the fabric with gel medium, using a bit of water and the brush.

ONE
Tear a Piece of Canvas

Tear out a workable piece of canvas by making a small cut at one end of the fabric and then tearing it.

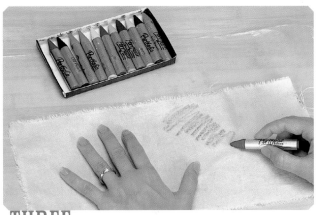

THREE
Color With Pastels

Scribble and make various marks, over the surface of the dried gel medium, with oil pastels.

FOUR
Add Water

Work the color into the canvas using your brush and water.

FIVE
Apply a Second Color

Try adding a second color for interest. I like to use at least two colors when I am staining the canvas.

SIX
Mask Off Stripes or Shapes

After the fabric has dried, create stripes or shapes by placing rows of masking tape onto the fabric.

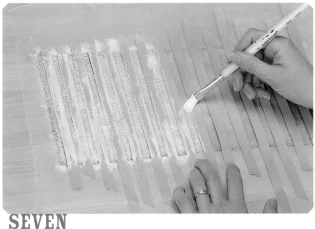

SEVEN
Paint Over the Tape

Then paint over the tape with acrylic paint. To prevent the paint from bleeding under the tape, a fairly dry brush works best.

Moment

What other shapes could you make on your fabric? Circles? Squares? Stars? Hearts? Create lettering using acrylic paint and a fine line brush.

What you will need

- photocopy ○ watercolor paper
- gel medium ○ paint brushes
- acrylic paints (including Titan Buff)
- scissors ○ color-stained fabric
- needle and thread ○ untreated canvas ○ rice (for filling) ○ fine point black pen ○ markers ○ cigar box
- craft knife ○ sandpaper ○ gesso
- acrylic sheeting ○ acrylic cutting tool ○ tissue paper ○ pencil
- doll house window ○ Elmer's Glue
- gum arabic ○ waxed paper
- spray bottle with water
- damp sponge ○ oil paints
- linseed oil ○ brayer ○ spoon

TEXTURAL TECHNIQUES

ELMER'S GLUE CRACKLE (PAGE 20)
...
SKETCHING INTO WET PAINT (PAGE 26)
...
TISSUE PAPER LAYER (PAGE 28)
...
PRINTING WITH ONE COLOR (PAGE 52)
...
COLOR-STAINED FABRIC (PAGE 62)

Once I Saw a Little Bird

(CIGAR BOX)

The figure element in this piece is a poppet doll. I will show you how you can create these charming dolls using the canvas that we prepared earlier. Make similar dolls using your family photos and set them on the mantle for a unique family portrait. My cats love these (they think I made special toys just for them) but so will you and your family!

In this project, I'll show you how you can add a text element to your own cigar box assemblage. You'll also have the opportunity to combine the techniques of sketching in paint, tissue paper, and Elmer's Glue crackle.

By using text as an element, you can add a touch of mystery to your collage projects. I like the way that this text suggests the beginning of a story and leads me to wonder what else happened after she saw the little bird.

What if your figure had accessories? Hat? Umbrella? What other kinds of heads could you use with the same doll? Cats? Birds? What if you attached arms using doll arms or other sculpted arms? What if you added more embellishments like ribbon or beads?

WHAT IF...

ONE
Mount Copy to Watercolor Paper

Start with two copies—one of a photo and the other of text. Adhere the photo to watercolor paper and position the text on top using gel medium.

TWO
Paint Over the Text

Go over the text with Titan Buff and allow the paint to dry. Add a second color over the Titan Buff.

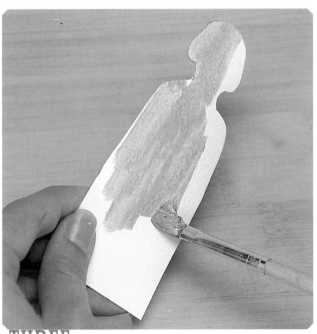

THREE
Cut Out the Figure

Cut the image out and then paint the front and back using acrylic paint. Here I chose green because I wanted it to match the green canvas I stained for her skirt.

FOUR
Measure For Skirt

Now you can measure your figure for her three-dimensional skirt. Make marks on the fabric on either side of your figure. Allow a little extra room for sewing a seam.

FIVE
Cut Out the Skirt

Fold the color-stained fabric and cut two layers of the skirt out at once. I don't worry about my skirt being perfect. I think they are more charming when they are a little asymetrical or off balance.

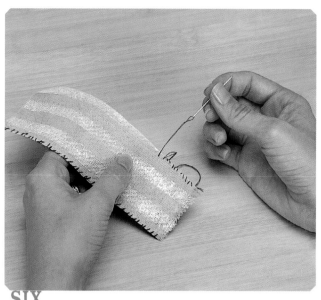

SIX
Sew Long Sides

Using the needle and thread, sew the two layers together along the sides.

SEVEN
Begin Skirt Bottom

Cut a rectangle of untreated canvas that is just a little bit wider than the skirt. Sew onto the edge of one side of the bottom of the skirt.

EIGHT
Force in the Side

Tuck in the opposite side of the rectangle and sew to the other side of the skirt bottom.

NINE
Fold in One Side

Stick a paintbrush into the open end of the skirt to expand the bottom. Tuck in one short side and sew to attach, then repeat on the opposite side.

TEN
Pour in the Rice

Pour rice into the finished skirt, leaving about 1½" (4cm) at the top of the skirt empty.

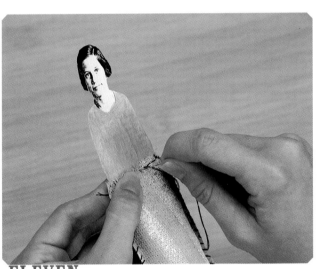

ELEVEN
Stitch the Skirt Closed

Insert your painted figure piece into the opening at the top of the skirt. Use a straight stitch to secure the figure into the skirt and sew the skirt shut.

TWELVE
Paint the Bottom

Paint the bottom of the skirt to match, and then add final details to the figure using the fine-point black pen. Use markers to add color.

THIRTEEN
Measure Using Lid

Prepare your cigar box as you did on page 37, by removing the lid, sanding then painting it with gesso. Set the box aside to dry. Take the lid and set it on top of your acrylic sheet. Mark with a pen along the length and width.

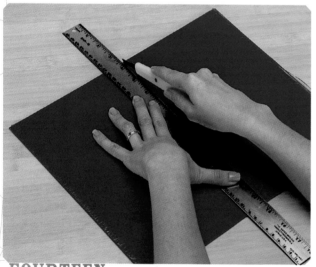

FOURTEEN
Score One Side

Using a ruler and an acrylic cutter, score along one of the marks. It is better to make lots of light scores because you'll have more control over the tool. I usually make about 10 swipes.

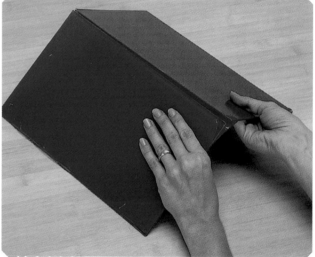

FIFTEEN
Snap Apart

After you have scored the sheet, snap it apart to break it. Then repeat scoring and breaking for the other line. Now you should have a piece of acrylic that will fit perfectly on your cigar box.

SIXTEEN
Add Tissue and Paint Inside Box

Apply a little gel medium to the back of the inside of the box, then cover it with tissue. Smoosh the tissue around to create texture. Allow the tissue to dry, then dry brush paint over the tissue and onto the sides. I have chosen a light yellow here.

SEVENTEEN
Sketch Into the Paint

Use a pencil to sketch out a composition in the wet tissue. You can experiment with making scribbles, words or random shapes. I like to do swirly shapes.

EIGHTEEN
Decide on Other Elements

Set your already-created poppet doll into the box to get an idea of what other elements you want to add. Go through your collage supplies and hold elements up until you find something you like. I thought a window would look good here.

What if you had two poppet dolls in the composition instead of one? Would you have combined different techniques together or used different colors? What if you were to use the plastic wrap or rinse aid techniques on the outside of the box?

WHAT IF...

NINETEEN
Doctor Up Your Pieces

Paint your elements to suit your own composition. Then hold them up to your box again to see what else needs to be done. I chose to paint my window with Yellow Ochre acrylic paint. Then I thought it needed a collage element behind it to add interest. Maybe a blue sky and a bird? I placed those elements under the window to see if they would look good.

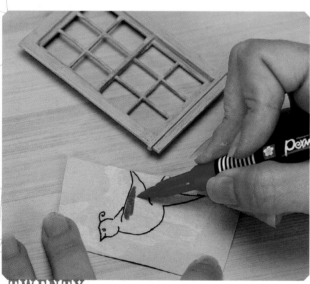

TWENTY
Add Additional Pieces

After deciding I liked the little bird, I glued it to the blue paper, using gel medium, and then I colored it red, to compliment the green poppet doll dress and bring out the red elements in her buttons and bow tie.

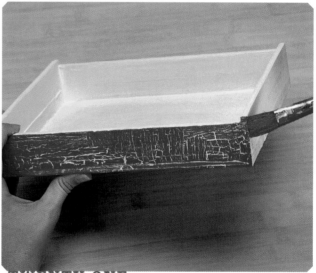

TWENTY-ONE
Add Crackle to Box Exterior

Before gluing in all of your elements, add texture to the outside of the box by applying an Elmer's Glue crackle in your chosen color. I settled on red as a good match for the bird.

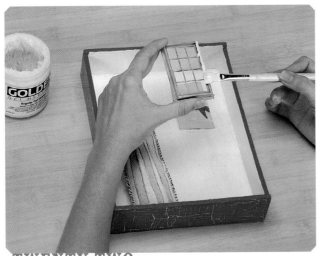

TWENTY-TWO
Assemble Elements Inside the Box

After the crackled paint is dry, glue your elements to the inside of the box. Here I am using gel medium to glue on my window. I also used gel medium to glue in my poppet doll.

TWENTY-THREE
Print Text Onto Acrylic Sheet

Hold your piece of acrylic over your finished box to decide the best placement for your text or other image. (Because we are transferring onto the back of the plexiglas, you do not need to reverse your image on the photocopier.) I liked the idea of having text in the lower-right corner. Text that mentioned a bird really helped to finish the story. Peel the backing off of one side of the acrylic. Using the spoon printing technique from pages 52–54, transfer your text or image to the exposed side of the acrylic sheet. You can mark on the protective coating where the placement will be. Because plastic is much less porous than fabric or paper, very little pressure is needed to transfer the image. Set the acrylic sheet in a clean place to dry for about a week.

TWENTY-FOUR
Glue Acrylic Sheet to Box

After it has dried, peel off the rest of the protective coating and make sure your box and acrylic are free of lint and dust. If you need to clean the acrylic with window cleaner, do so very carefully around your printed image. Apply gel medium to the edges at the top and bottom of the box and glue the acrylic sheet into place.

What you will need

○ photocopy ○ unstretched, unprimed canvas ○ gum arabic ○ waxed paper ○ spray bottle with water ○ damp sponge ○ palette paper ○ oil paint ○ linseed oil ○ brayer ○ spoon or pasta machine ○ gel medium ○ water-soluble oil pastels ○ acrylic paint ○ circle sponge applicator ○ embroidery thread and needle ○ canvas pad ○ Elmer's Glue-All ○ 1-inch (25mm) brush ○ scissors ○ buttons ○ fine point pen ○ popsicle stick

TEXTURAL TECHNIQUES

ELMER'S GLUE CRACKLE (PAGE 20)
...
PRINTING WITH ONE COLOR (PAGE 52)
...
COLOR-STAINED FABRIC (PAGE 62)

Clever Judy!

(CANVAS WALL HANGING)

Clever Judy! Why does she think she's so smart? Probably because she's a really snazzy wall hanging that will add sizzle to any room!

This collage project gives you an opportunity to practice printmaking onto fabric, color staining unprimed canvas, and incorporating Elmer's Glue crackle for a crowning finish!

ONE
Make a Print

Make a one-color print from your photocopy onto a piece of unprimed canvas.

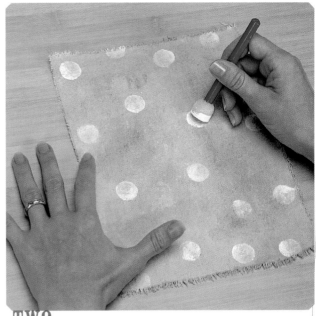

TWO
Paint the Canvas

Prepare a second piece of canvas with water and oil pastels. Using paint and a sponge applicator, apply white polka dots to the painted canvas.

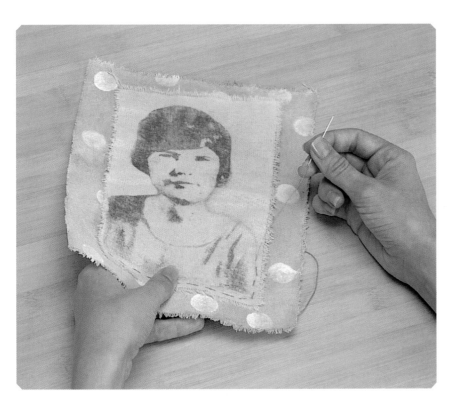

THREE
Sew Print to Canvas

Choose a color of embroidery thread and sew the fabric print onto the polka dot canvas, using a running stitch. I chose orange so it would be a near match to the red without repeating it exactly.

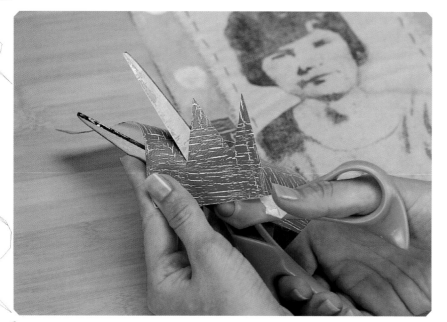

FOUR
Create a Crackle Crown

Create crackle on a piece of canvas pad, with Elmer's Glue and acrylic paint. When it is dry, cut out a shape of a crown or a hat for the head of your figure. I also added a little bit of text to the crown.

FIVE
Attach the Crown

Adhere the crown to the head of the figure, using gel medium.

SIX
Sew on Notions

Sew a couple of buttons onto the shirt of the figure. I used turquoise buttons to play off the color of the crown.

SEVEN
Sew Around Three Sides

Sew a running stitch around three sides of the canvas, leaving the top unstitched. At the top, leave slack in the thread for a hanging loop, then tie it off at the opposite corner, on the back.

EIGHT
Add Final Details

Embellish the crown if you want to, and then add details with a fine point pen.

NINE
Add a Stick for Support

If your piece sags in the center when you suspend it by the hanger, you can glue a popsicle stick to the back for support.

What you will need

○ 12" × 12" (30cm × 30cm) prestretched canvas ○ acrylic paints ○ paint brushes ○ plastic wrap ○ decorative punch (optional) ○ scissors ○ contact paper ○ unstretched, unprimed canvas ○ photocopy ○ gum arabic ○ waxed paper ○ spray bottle with water ○ damp sponge ○ palette paper ○ oil paints ○ linseed oil ○ brayers, 2 ○ spoon or pasta machine ○ gel medium ○ water-soluble oil pastels ○ button or large bead ○ fine point pen ○ embroidery thread and needle ○ masking tape ○ ribbon

TEXTURAL TECHNIQUES

PLASTIC WRAP CRINKLE (PAGE 22)
...
CONTACT PAPER SHAPES (PAGE 32)
...
LAYERING MULTIPLE PRINTS (PAGE 57)
...
COLOR-STAINED FABRIC (PAGE 62)

Snappy Kate

(FABRIC BOOK ON CANVAS)

I enjoy working in altered books, but when I have finished, it's difficult to figure out how to display them. Do I display them on a table? On a bookshelf? It's always a dilemma. I enjoy the intimacy of creating in a book, but then I also enjoy the ease of display that a 2-D format provides.

In this next project I'll show you how you can have your cake and eat it too! We'll create a book on a canvas background using unprimed canvas or fabric. When you have completed your book, you'll be able to hang it on a wall for display, or take it down to have a peek inside.

To create this "snappy" piece, we'll be combining plastic wrap, contact paper shapes, and printing onto fabric.

What if Kate wore a different hat? What if there were different words on the cover? How might it change the mood of the piece? What other techniques could you use instead? Masking tape? Elmer's Glue crackle? What if you created a much bigger canvas with a grouping of books on the same piece?

WHAT IF...

ONE
Create Plastic Wrap Texture

Complete the plastic wrap texture on a prestretched canvas and allow the paint to dry, then remove the plastic wrap.

TWO
Add Contact Shapes

Cut shapes from contact paper and add them to the painted canvas. Paint over the contact paper shapes with another color. After the paint has dried, peel off the contact paper. Here I layered a sage green color over the yellow. I decided that I wanted to start with a soft color so that I could give myself room to go darker if I wanted to later.

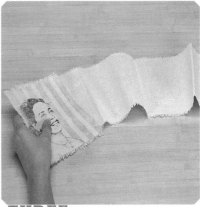

THREE
Prepare Book Fabric

Tear a piece of unprimed canvas down to a size that will look good centered on your canvas. This will be the cover of your book. Create a layered print on this piece. Here, I used a striped background and a figure. Cut a second piece of fabric that is the same height as the cover by four times the width of the cover.

FOUR
Add Color to Fabric

Set the cover aside and prepare the long piece of fabric by first priming it with gel medium, and then adding color with water and oil pastel. I thought I would play off the pink in the cover and create pink pages.

FIVE
Add Embellishments to Cover

Color both sides of the fabric, and set aside to dry. While you are waiting for the interior of the book to dry, add embellishments or other details to your cover. Be sure and use at least one button or large bead in the center of the right hand side of the cover. This will be used for the closure later on.

SIX
Add Pen Details

Cut out additional elements from paper if you wish and apply them to the cover with gel medium. I wanted to add a tiara to my gal. It looked like she needed one. Add additional details, such as jewelry, with a fine point pen.

SEVEN
Pierce the Two Signatures

Use the cover as a guide to fold the long piece of fabric into four sections. Cut to separate at the middle fold. Now you should have two pieces, each with a fold down the middle.

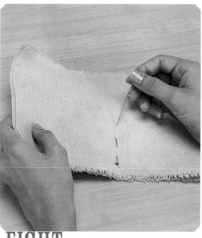

EIGHT
Stitch Signatures Together

Lay the two pieces on top of each other, then stitch together down the center with a simple running stitch. Now you have a little book!

NINE
Glue on the Cover

Using gel medium, glue the completed cover to the front page of the book.

TEN
Add Text

For a finishing touch, add a line of text to the cover and outline it in pen. I chose this saying because it seemed funny to me, and made me ask questions about the woman on the cover. Maybe she had won her tiara for her snappy remarks? Maybe she was a beauty queen and she was snippy to the other contestants?

ELEVEN
Mask Around the Booklet

Decorate and embellish the interior however you like. Then place the booklet in the center of the canvas. Mask around it using masking tape.

TWELVE
Paint in Masked Area

Remove the booklet and then paint inside the masked square with acrylic paint. Remove the tape and let the paint dry. I chose to paint my square blue, to play off the blue in the cover.

THIRTEEN
Glue Booklet to Canvas

Using gel medium, glue the back page of the booklet to the painted square in the center of the canvas.

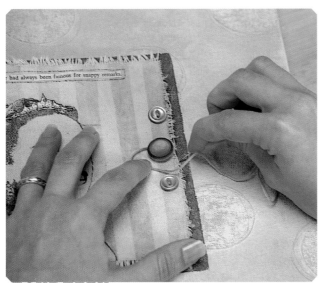

FOURTEEN
Add a Closure

With coordinating embroidery thread, sew a small loop through the canvas to keep the booklet closed. Start at the back of the canvas and come up near the center button, loosely wrap the thread around the button and then go back down through the canvas. You could use elastic thread or ribbon as a closure, too.

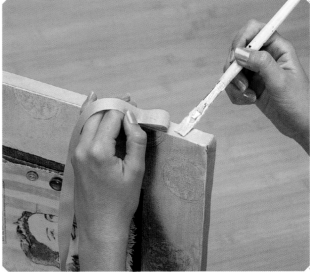

FIFTEEN
Finish the Edges

Finish off the edges of the canvas with ribbon. After I had finished my canvas, I decided that the dots needed to be lighter to make them show at a distance. I adjusted them with a dry brush and a dab of white acrylic paint. Do you have any finishing touches or changes you'd like to make to your piece?

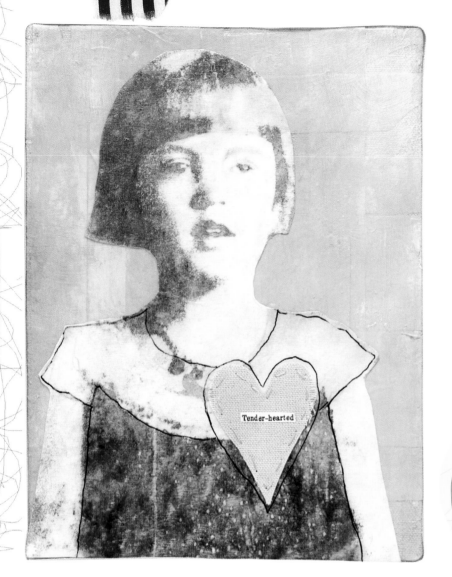

TEXTURAL TECHNIQUES

LAYERED MASKING TAPE (PAGE 24)
· · ·
PRINTING WITH ONE COLOR (PAGE 52)
· · ·
COLOR-STAINED FABRIC (PAGE 62)

Tenderhearted
(CANVAS)

This tenderhearted girl combines masking tape and printmaking. Sometimes you don't need to have a lot of collage elements to tell your story. Do you have a powerful image that you would like to use as a centerpiece on your canvas? Grab your copies and your masking tape, and let's get started!

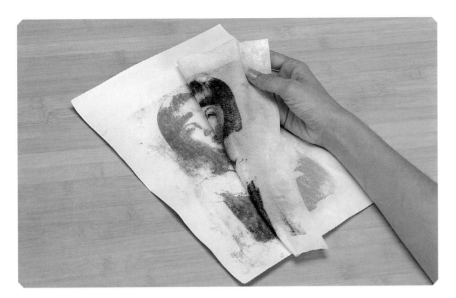

ONE
Create a Print

Create a print using the spoon method on a piece of watercolor paper. Here I printed an image of a little girl, using Burnt Umber oil paint.

TWO
Cut Out the Figure

When it is dry, cut out the figure from the watercolor paper.

THREE
Add Tape Texture to Canvas

Create a layered masking tape background in the color of your choice.

FOUR
Add Figure to Canvas

Using gel medium, glue the figure to the textured canvas.

FIVE
Try Out Elements

If you want to add an element like a fabric heart, but you're not sure what color you want it, cut out a few options and try them on for size. At first I tried yellow, then green but finally settled on pink. The green felt too close to blue and the yellow didn't look too hot next to the brown, so pink was the answer!

SIX
Fray the Fabric

Try roughing up the fabric a bit by fraying it. I find it easiest to use a pin to pull out the threads.

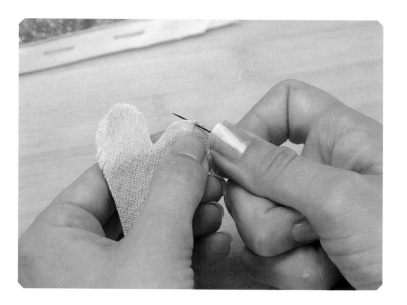

SEVEN
Sew on Fabric Elements

Sew the heart onto the canvas with embroidery thread, using a running stitch around its perimeter. You may want to experiment with the best placement for the heart. It will be much easier to sew the heart on if you punch holes ahead of your sewing with a tack or safety pin.

EIGHT
Add Text and Pen Details

Glue text onto the heart, using gel medium, and then add details here and there with a fine point pen.

NINE
Finish Off With Ribbon

Finish off the sides with ribbon if you like.

BRINGING PERSONAL IMAGERY INTO YOUR ARTWORK

THE MORE PERSONAL WE CAN MAKE OUR ARTWORK, THE MORE IT MEANS TO OUR FAMILY AND TO US.

What could be more personal than using your own photos and drawings in your collages?

Ah, so you say you can't draw? I say—yes, you can! If you can put pen to paper, then you can draw. Maybe your drawings don't resemble a photograph, but isn't that what we have cameras for?

When I look at other artists' work, it's the quirky and honest quality of the line work that excites me. Not the fact that they made a bowl of fruit or a sunset look "just like the real thing." I am more interested in their unique hand and personal touch.

Our world is now almost completely computerized and digital. Computers create things that are flat, with no bumps. Everything is smooth and perfect. Isn't it refreshing to have something quirky, off-center and—best of all—created by you?

In this next section I'll show you how to use your own photos in your collages. Photos of your family, friends and even pets. I'll also show you how to become more comfortable with using your own drawing and linework in your collages, along with exercises to practice and tips you can use right away.

USING YOUR OWN CURRENT PHOTOS

You might have a photo with two people together, and you'd prefer to use them as separate elements in a composition. Here's how I prepare my photos for collage.

ONE
Make Copies of Your Photos

Select several of your favorite photos and make black and white copies of them, reducing their size. Cut your images to separate them from the background, so that you have just the heads trimmed out.

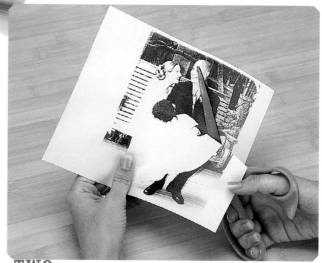

TWO
Choose Two Figures in the Same Photo

If you would like to use two figures from the same photo, sometimes you need to do a little surgery. First trim around both figures using scissors.

THREE
Cut the Two Figures Apart

Then trim between the figures and around facial features using a craft knife. Be careful! You'd be surprised how different someone can look when just 1 millimeter of his nose goes missing!

FOUR
Replace Cut-Off Body Sections

After your images are cut apart, glue them onto watercolor paper and then add in any sections of the bodies that are missing, such as shoulders. Since I had to cut off part of Paul's shoulders from the photo, I can add it back in at this time to make him the manly man that he is.

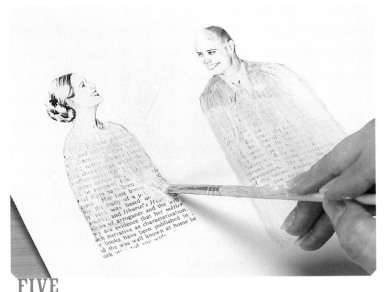

FIVE
Add Text, Then Tone Down

Add some text or other patterned paper over the torso of the images, using gel medium. Tone the text down with Titan Buff acrylic paint.

Moment

What different varieties of text can you use? Try telling a story with the text on your figures. Perhaps handwriting their life story yourself or printing it out on the computer? If you were creating a collage for your uncle who is a math professor, wouldn't it be fun to incorporate numbers on his chest? What other elements could you use?

ADDING HAND-DRAWN ELEMENTS

Try practicing drawings on index cards. I pick a theme and see how many designs I can come up with using that theme. Here are a few cards that I created with hat and shoe themes.

I like to practice using a permanent fine point marker to build my drawing confidence. If a line doesn't go where I want it, I work to make it fit into the design. Try creating cards of your own and use them as a reference when you need ideas.

What you will need

○ Photocopies ○ Opaque markers ○ Fine tip pen

Here's an easy way to practice adding hand-drawn elements to your collage photos. Make a few black and white photocopies, grab a pen and your imagination and jump in. It's only a photocopy. Don't be shy! Soon you'll forget that you are "drawing" and you'll feel like you are in grade school, drawing on the textbook photos. The only difference is that now we get to call it art! Here, I am adding pizzazz to Marcus the Cat, but you could do this on any photo—friends, family or foe!

ONE
Draw a Half Circle
Begin with a half circle on top of the head.

TWO
Use Opaque Pen in Dark Spots
If areas of the figure are dark, color them in with a white gel pen or opaque marker.

THREE
Create a Rim
Make a little rim.

FOUR
Add Sections
Add in the sections of the hat.

FIVE
Finish With Propeller
Then add a little propeller on the top to complete.

SIX
Brighten With Color
It's fun to add a touch of color to your finished sketches. Notice the three other hats I gave to Marcus? What types of hats can you come up with? Think about how each hat could be broken into simple geometric elements. Most hats consist of circles or squares.

CREATING A NARRATIVE PHOTO COLLAGE

Narrative collages are a series of artworks (usually two or more) that tell a story. I think of mine as film stills or storyboards that represent a moment in time.

You can create a narrative collage by telling a story about a memory or event. Try to look past the obvious. Extract a sliver of time and honor it by creating a series of collages centered around that event.

Pick a Theme

To get started you'll need to begin with a general theme. In my case, I wanted to do a piece about my mother and myself.

Brainstorm to dig out memories that will help to tell a story about your life. Begin with a list of all the items you can think of in relation to your topic. Try to be as specific as possible. If you are doing a piece about your mother, start with your earliest memory of her. Was there anything she used to say over and over again? Did she have any nicknames for you? Funny birthday party memories? How about her favorite dessert? There are no rules. Simply make lists of all the memories that come to you. Here are a few of my childhood memories from my first brainstorming list:

• reading together in the afternoon on rainy days

• eating noodle soup on the floor on moving day

• coming back to Mom after a day in kindergarten

• Mom desperately trying to get me to eat something healthy

• feeding geese and having them run after us when we ran out of bread

Narrow Your Topic

From the list in the first column, I selected the subject that strikes me as the most interesting. They all have potential but the topic of "Mom desperately trying to get me to eat something healthy" stands out for me. I have so many memories of my mother's endless trials in getting me to eat. Next I created a list of ideas from that topic, starting with a list of items that I *would* eat:

• macaroni and cheese

• breaded chicken

• scrambled eggs

• apple juice

• sliced apples

• toast

While writing this list, I wondered how Mom might have felt cooking the same dishes over and over again. I imagined her musing as she cooked yet another slice of chicken breast in breadcrumbs—wondering how many times she had made the recipe before (probably thousands).

This struck me as a really interesting angle and a funny way to depict a fragment of our lives. I had found my topic! I decided my tribute would be: My mom, and how many times she had cooked chicken, not because she wanted to, but because she loved me.

Composition

Once you have a theme, it is time to think about how the compositions might be arranged. My narrative is in sections so I will create a triptych, or a three-part collage. As I dig through my photographs, I lay each one out on my canvases and play with them until I find an arrangement that fits. As I experiment with the photographs, I also try to think about what colors to use in my composition.

If you do not want to use actual photos, make black and white copies at your local copy center. Also, don't feel that you are limited to using only photo images in your collage. You can incorporate pieces of clothing or fabric, letters, jew-

elry, etc. Use anything that you feel will add to your piece and help to tell the story.

I began my story with a photograph of me as a child. I tore out chicken recipes from an old cookbook, tinted them orange and cut the pieces into house shapes. For the middle canvas I used a copy of a calendar page and trimmed it into a house shape to represent all of the many days that I ate the same meal. On the third canvas, I chose a copied image of my mother. I experimented with placing a hand-drawn image of an oven behind her. The page that the oven is drawn on is a paragraph about English cooking—perfect! (My mother is English.) I gave my mom an apron from a fabric remnant. I have a clear memory of her wearing an apron like that and cooking chicken for me when we visited my grandma in England. I like the way that she appears as though she really is thinking about how many times she's cooked chicken!

All of the elements have a special meaning and relate to my memories. To complete my story, I added typed words to my canvases.

Of course, your narrative collage will be very different, using your own imagery and your memories. As you are working, ask questions to hone in on your subject matter and be as specific as possible. Below is a list of prompts that might help you discover memories for your collages.

People

• Are there any clichés that this person used to say?

• Nicknames they had or that they would call you?

• What was your average day like with this person? Or what was their day like?

• Any routines they would always do? Black coffee every morning, or reading the paper out loud?

• Smells can be very evocative. What smells make you think of this person?

• Are there any family words, or made-up words that only your family uses?

• Does the person have a favorite tie or dress, or way of wearing their hair?

Places

Your childhood home:

   • Were you afraid of the basement?

   • What was your favorite room?

   • What color was your bedroom?

   • Did you play outside or inside?

   • What dolls or toys did you prefer?

   • Did you have slumber parties?

Homes you've lived in:

   • Your first home as an adult

   • Your dorm room from college

   • Your first apartment

Cities you've lived in or visited:

   • Smells of the city

   • Restaurants you've eaten in

   • Hotel or vacation stories

Time

Pick a year in your life and try to remember every detail. Start with January and work your way through. Try to recall tiny things and simple pleasures. Lunch with a friend, a lazy afternoon nap, how you felt after a new haircut.

Create a narrative collage using images of a family member at different times in their life: baby, child, young adult. Ask them what they remember, or focus in on what you recall about them at each stage in their life. Try to select one memory for each life-stage.

LEARNING TO LOOSEN UP!

Try this exercise to really get out of your drawing shell and embrace imperfection!

Use your non-dominant hand (for me, it's my left) and practice drawing various elements. Here I am drawing a house and a tree. Writing with your non-dominant hand is a great way to create funky, child-like lettering. In this example I was so wrapped up in concentrating on my hand movements that I misspelled "sweet". So get ready to embrace your inner, uncoordinated self and give it a shot!

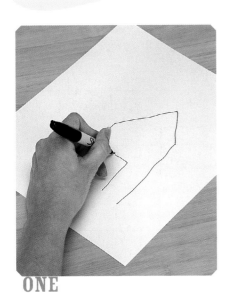

ONE
House

First, try a simple house.

TWO
Tree

Then add a tree next to it.

THREE
Practice Writing Words

Practice writing words too—it's hard!

What you will need

○ copies of your photos
○ 12" × 12" (30cm × 30xm)
canvas ○ acrylic paints ○ paint
brush ○ masking tape ○ markers
○ gel medium ○ fabric for outfits
○ graphite transfer paper
○ fine point ink pen
○ kneaded eraser ○ ribbon

TEXTURAL TECHNIQUES

SKETCHING INTO WET PAINT (PAGE 26)
...
USING YOUR OWN CURRENT PHOTOS (PAGE 86)
...
ADDING HAND-DRAWN ELEMENTS (PAGE 88)

Family Portrait
(CANVAS)

When working with photos in collage, we are used to creating artwork around Victorian or other nostalgic images. So how do we work our current photos into a composition? I'll show you how I did it and then you can adapt my methods to your work. You can include your pets, too!

Even when I am working on a personalized piece of artwork, I don't plan it out in advance. I prefer to allow the piece to evolve and "tell me" where it wants to go. As I create the collage that follows, I'll let you know what I am thinking as I move from one step to the next. I invite you to ask similar questions and try composition variations as you work on your own collages.

ONE
Experiment With Composition

Lay out your elements on your canvas and play around with them to decide on the best composition. For the first composition, I experimented with placing Paul and me on either side of the canvas with the pets in the center. When I looked at this, it didn't feel right. It felt as though our pets separated us and I wanted us to feel like a family unit, so I tried another composition.

TWO
Try Another Version

In this version, I experimented with placing Paul and me on one side and the pets on the other, but again, it didn't read as if we are a family unit. The pets seemed outside our relationship and that wasn't the feeling I was going for.

THREE
Decide on Final Composition

For the final arrangement, I placed Paul and me in the center, with Toby at Paul's side and the kitties by my feet. Now this composition feels right!

FOUR
Add Sketch in Wet Paint

After deciding on a final composition, cover the canvas with your color of choice and then lightly sketch your composition with a pencil into the wet paint. Here I chose a light yellow color as the background, and since I am doing a family portrait, I thought it would be fun to have a large house shape.

FIVE
Mask Off, Then Paint

Mask off the main shape, which here happens to be a house, and then paint in the background outside of the masked line. I used Cobalt Teal acrylic paint to fill in the sky or background.

SIX
Outline Main Shape

After everything is dry, remove the masking tape. Outline your main shape with a colored pen or paint. Here, I outlined the house in a "stitch" of red, using an opaque marker.

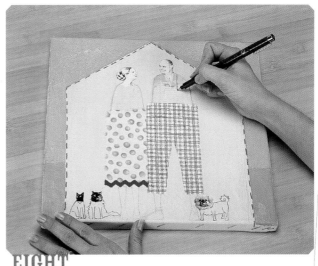

SEVEN
Add Clothes and Details

Glue in your figures and give them some fabric clothes. Sketch out your pets' bodies on separate paper so you can practice until you are happy with your design. Then transfer them to the canvas with graphite transfer paper.

EIGHT
Sharpen Transfers With Pen

Dab at the transferred areas with a kneaded eraser to soften them, then go over your transfers with a fine point pen. I also added a little thought bubble for Toby and hats for the kitties.

NINE
Add Color With Marker

Make finishing touches with a colored marker. Then finish the edges of your canvas with ribbon.

What you will need

○ copies of current photo(s)
○ scissors ○ watercolor paper
○ gel medium ○ acrylic paints
○ paint brushes ○ cigar box
(lid removed) ○ gesso ○ pencil
○ colored cardstock ○ fine point
pen ○ graphite transfer paper
○ mini wooden spools

TEXTURAL TECHNIQUES

SKETCHING INTO WET PAINT (PAGE 26)
· · ·
USING YOUR OWN CURRENT PHOTOS (PAGE 86)
· · ·
ADDING HAND-DRAWN ELEMENTS (PAGE 88)

A Not-So-Rainy Day
(CIGAR BOX)

When I was a little girl, I remember what a big deal it was to get my first umbrella. I couldn't wait for it to rain so I could use it. When it hadn't rained for a few days, I became very tired of waiting so I went outside and held my new umbrella proudly above my head as I walked around in the bright sunshine.

When I was asked to create an artwork on commission by the mother of this little girl, I thought of my own experience and adapted it into a collage for her. I think she looks pretty snazzy with her umbrella and hot pink rain boots.

What other elements could be in the background? Birds? A bicycle? What if she had a different outfit, such as pants or shorts? How would different shoes change the feel of the piece?

WHAT IF...

ONE
Cut Figure Out of Copy

Make a copy of your photo and then cut out the figure(s) you wish to use. For this project I will only be using the little girl.

TWO
Add Desired Body Parts

Glue the copy onto watercolor paper, using gel medium and then glue text on top. Add a bit of paint to tone down the text, and then add an arm or other body parts that you wish to use to tell a story. Don't worry about making things look perfect or realistic. Here, I gave my girl an arm so that she could hold an umbrella.

THREE
Decide on a Composition

Cover your box with gesso and let it dry. Arrange your elements on the box to figure out a composition and what colors to use for the background.

FOUR
Sketch In the Scenery

Add your chosen paint to the background and, with a pencil, sketch in some hills or other things of scenic interest. I thought adding hills would be nice, since she is outside on her rainy day.

FIVE
Compare Clothing Options

Paint the inside sides of the box as well. Set your figure in the box and then hold up different papers to compare options for clothes. I liked the way the pink and brown polka dotted paper played off the blue background.

SIX
Add Boots and Legs

Cut out the clothes and glue them to your figure. On different paper, draw boots or legs and shoes.

SEVEN
Glue Figure Pieces Together

Cut out the boots, leaving a little tab at the top with which to glue them to the underside of the skirt. Paint the tab portion a color if you like, to peek through as a leg between the boot and the skirt. Glue all of the figure pieces together using gel medium. I decided to make her leg kick up slightly. It makes her look cute and sassy. Experiment with moving the legs around before gluing them down to see if it changes the feel of your figure.

EIGHT
Add More Paper Elements

You can glue in papers to add color. Instead of painting the umbrella, I cut out a polka dot paper shape and glued it down using gel medium.

NINE
Add Details With Pen

Finish your figure off with fine point pen details.

TEN
Glue in Background Elements

Place the figure back in the box to decide the best placement and to see if you are inspired to add any supporting elements like birds or maybe houses in the background. Here, I thought a row of houses would be nice. Glue in these elements.

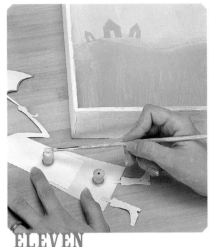

ELEVEN
Add Mini Spools to Figure

Glue wooden mini spools to the back of the figure so that it will be raised up. Place the figure back in the box to double check the placement and then apply gel medium to the back of the spools to glue the figure in the box.

TWELVE
Draw From a Reference

I thought this little girl looked lonely and needed a doggie friend. For additional elements, such as this dog, it is easier to draw if you have a reference, like I did with this sticker book. Or you can trace illustrations from a book if you want to.

THIRTEEN
Cut Out Final Elements

Cut out these last elements and paint them, then outline with a fine point pen. I gave the dog polka dots so he'd match the girl.

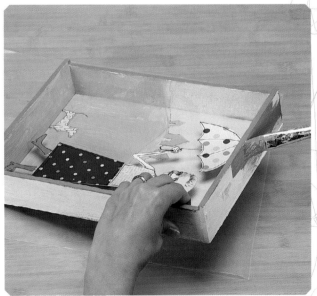

FOURTEEN
Paint the Box Exterior

Glue them into the box and add any last details with the pen or markers. Paint the outside of the box with a coordinating color and you're done!

desolate
he last
Castle. My father,
was Master of the
secretary to Lo
cond term as Lo
My mother, the
District Inspector of
en sisters celebrated
Miss

shoe queen

THE POWER OF COLOR

WHEN YOU SIT DOWN TO BEGIN A NEW ARTWORK, HOW DO YOU DECIDE WHAT COLORS TO USE?

Do you grab the first tube of paint you see and work from there? Do you find yourself reaching for the same colors over and over again? It can be difficult to pull color combinations off the top of your head. As artists, we are visual people, so we need visual clues as to what colors work together. We need reference!

I keep a color journal where I save clippings from magazines and catalogs. These are visual prompts to remind me which color combinations I prefer. Then when it's time to make new artwork, I can flip through my color journal and pick out a page with samples that I like. In the end, I might veer away from the original inspiration, but at least it's a start!

You can use anything to inspire your color choices: cutouts from clothing and furniture catalogs, a piece of fabric that you like, paint chips, wallpaper samples, your own photos and so on.

In the following two exercises, I have created a series of collages, each around the same color palette. I'll show you how I arrived at my color choices and how I used them in each piece. I hope you'll begin to keep a color journal of your own and use it to explore new combinations. There is a whole wide world of color out there—so let's get started!

Scheme I
(TEAL, GREEN, RED & PINK)

I love the colors teal and red together—so yummy! However, I have been using those colors together over and over, and it is becoming mundane. To encourage myself to mix things up a bit, I clipped colors from magazines until I found a new twist to my favorite combination. Looking at my clippings, I noticed that I enjoyed the green dots on the teal background as well as the way pink and red looked with the teal. I pasted everything in my color journal to use as reference.

Before beginning my artwork, I studied my color clippings. I preferred teal as the dominant color and the red, pink and green worked better as accent colors. With that as my guide, I began my collages, allowing the teal to be the background color in all three of the artworks.

You might notice that in each collage, the accent colors (pink, red and green) are in varying degrees of dominance. Simply by switching out prominent colors, you can expand the look of your color palette.

By using magazine cutouts as my inspiration, I managed to find a color palette that I had never tried before. Experiment with cutting out magazine pages as I did, and then challenge yourself to explore something new!

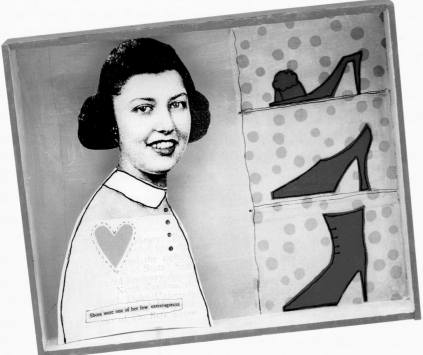

SHOES—ONE OF HER FEW EXTRAVAGANCES
…On this cigar box, I used pink polka-dotted tissue as a background with red shoes on top. I repeated red in the woman's buttons to bring just a hint of color to the left side of the piece. Pink was repeated in the heart on the woman's chest as well. To complete the work, I painted the frame of the cigar box in green.

HOME …I used a touch of pink in the woman's polka-dotted skirt on this canvas. I allowed red to be the dominant accent color by using it in her shoes, heart, the frame of the house, the house outside and on the bird. Notice how the red acts as a guide, leading your eye around the artwork?

I THOUGHT SHE HAD BETTER TASTE …For this canvas, I used the magazine clipping of green dots on the teal background as reference for the background. I placed two girls on top, both wearing red dresses with pink accents, one with a pink tiara and the other with a pink button. In this piece the pink is the least dominant color, but there's still enough to add some zing.

Scheme II
(PINK, LIME GREEN, YELLOW & ORANGE)

The inspiration for the palette in these collages was a pair of socks that I found at a gift shop. I bought them simply because I loved the way the colors went together. Following my theory that you can use just about anything for color reference, I decided to give it a shot and use the sock color palette in a series of collages.

Before I began, I studied the socks and the arrangement of colors. I noted that the background color was a soft yellow which allowed all of the other colors to stand as accents without being overpowering. I made sure to do the same in my collages, using the soft yellow as a background in each piece and allowing the pink, lime green and orange to range in dominance as accent colors.

This pair of socks had dark hot pink in it as well. I felt that it was too busy to use five colors. I decided to allow the pink to be a "free color" that could be either dark or light in each composition. When you are using an item as a color inspiration, it should simply serve as a jumping off point and not as a rigid guideline. Don't be afraid to make changes as you see fit. You're the artist and you get to decide which colors to use!

Notice how, in each piece, the accent colors are in varying degrees of dominance? By rotating colors that play larger roles, you can broaden your palette range.

Simply by finding a pair of socks at the store, I wound up with a whole new color palette that I had never tried before. What can you find to use as color inspiration? Just about anything will do. Challenge yourself to get out of your usual color ruts and explore something different!

COOKING ...In this cigar box assemblage, pink is the dominant accent color, while orange makes only a small appearance.

BUNNY MAN AND THE TV ...On this canvas, orange is a very small accent color and green is allowed to dominate.

SMALL FEET ...In the collage of the man and his dog, the pink is barely there—only in the man's buttons and the dog's party hat, while orange is the dominant accent color.

COLLAGE CHALLENGE

THEY SAY THAT CREATIVITY CRAVES CHALLENGES. AND I HAVE TO AGREE!

I find nothing more exciting than a creative problem to tackle. I thought it would be exciting to extend a "collage challenge" to a few mixed-media artists and find out how they would tackle a project.

The theme for this collage challenge was Accessories and Necessities. I encouraged each artist to interpret this concept however she liked. There were only two rules: one, the artists had to use collage materials and two, their surface was to be some sort of hard case bought from the thrift store. It could be an old suitcase, makeup case, hard purse, etc.

Along with each artist's work you'll find her thoughts about the process, how she went about creating the work, what happened along the way and what sparked her ideas. As you read the artist's thought process, think about how it applies to your way of working on your creative projects.

Notice how each artist brings her unique vision to the challenge and allows the artwork to evolve during the creation process. Not one of us had a clear idea of where to start and in some cases the projects took on a life of their own and even surprised the creator!

So just how many different ways can one theme be interpreted? Well, let's find out!

Game of Life

LESLEY RILEY

My first objective was to find a little luggage case that inspired me. The case itself would set the stage for whatever I planned to do. The first one I found was an old roller skate carry case covered with stickers from roller rinks around the East Coast. It was colorful, but too big, and I stared at it for months waiting for inspiration—nothing came.

On my beach vacation I went to my favorite antique store and spied a little art deco doll trunk. It was radiating and I just knew this was *the* one. Ideas were firing off even before I paid for it. I felt like I had found a secret treasure. The next day I found a vintage photo of flapper girls. It all clicked—a game—with the flappers as the game pieces, moving around the board acquiring the Necessities and Accessories of life. The whole concept quickly fell into place. The hardest part would be designing the game board so that it would fold up to fit inside the case. I played around with that for the next month as I cut out my flappers and collected old checkers for the game tokens.

All the time I was thinking of a hard game *board*, but as the deadline approached it suddenly dawned on me that I should be thinking fabric. As a fabric artist, it is my primary medium. Sometimes the obvious just takes a little longer to arrive! Once I thought to use fabric for the game board, the rest of the work fell into place—a black felt background with colorful squares of fabric which all folded neatly into the case. I tried to keep the 1920s flapper theme going by using red, black and white and having the checks play off the pattern on the case. Once it was complete, I thought this project turned out exactly the way I had envisioned it when I found the perfect case—I wouldn't do anything differently!

To see more of Lesley's artwork, visit:
www.lalasland.com

Spirit Journey

KAREN MICHEL

The case I chose to work with was originally a hand-me-down from a friend of my mother's. I liked the shape and size of it. It was like a miniature suitcase. I envisioned some woman using it years ago on a vacation to bring along her jewels and makeup.

When I entered this project, I had to consider what the two concepts, *accessories* and *necessities* meant to me. Thinking symbolically of their meanings, I came to realize that what I hold as *accessories* are really items for my daily rituals, things that adorn my life. What I hold as *necessities* are elements my spirit requires for survival. Once I grasped my interpretation, I became excited! I then began to pretend that I was packing for a mystical journey, and every journey needs the proper luggage, right?

For accessories for the spirit, I lined the interior with horoscope pages, adding "celestial insight" as an accessory. I also added elements from the beach, where I feel most at home: a used beach pass, smoothed beach rocks and shells. A mirror served as a reminder for reflection and, of course, paint and brushes symbolize creation—all to accessorize and channel the ocean spirit.

Necessities for the spirit are simply defined by a burning heart milagro I purchased from a Mexican import store—a symbol of both passion and compassion and an image of the moon as a reminder of the bigger picture—divinity, the natural rhythm of the universe. Those two concepts, love and divinity, were really all that was necessary in my heart and mind.

Since this is a journey, a travel journal is needed to chronicle the adventures and lessons learned. I built the book and divided it into two chapters—Necessities and Accessories, of course. The pages are actual travel maps layered with bits and pieces from my other journals.

The overall case is a combination of objects collected, created and once used, so it is infused with personal meaning. Using archetypal symbology throughout, I hoped to achieve a universal interpretation of accessories and necessities.

To see more of Karen's artwork visit:
www.karenmichel.com

Bedrock TV

NINA BAGLEY

· ·

When Claudine invited me to create an art piece for her book, I dove with great gusto into my stash of vintage containers to see which sort of case would best suit this project. My first choice was the very one now portrayed on these pages; what was *not* in my plan was the look and feel that this quirky piece decided to exhibit!

My first plan for this artwork was to reflect an earthy feel and include assorted accessories of nature: riverbed stones, small driftwood, and some bare twiggy branches from the woods beside the river. I had an idea to display a transparent image of a water scene sandwiched between thin sheets of mica inside the case. A small low-wattage bulb could light it from within for dreamy night-time display. Then, across the image, I wanted to overlay the haunting words from a W. S. Merwin poem about a river: ". . . for every real lock, there is only one real key, and it's in some other dream, now invisible; it's the key to the one real door, it opens the water and sky both at once . . ."

Wonderful! My vision seemingly solid and squarely mapped, I began by cutting a large window in the panel, providing a frame for mica that would allow light to spill into the box. I glued one of my photographs of frost-covered trees to the back of the inside wall. I removed the white plastic handle and replaced it with wired driftwood and drilled, stacked stones threaded onto wire. Next came the feet, using more stones. (Could this project really be moving along as smoothly as it seemed?) For small twig branches, I used narrow strips of vintage barkcloth scraps, applying them almost as one would use strips of tape. I liked the way the scraps blended in nicely with the background tree images. Bravo! Simple!

While the production process was surprisingly easy, what became difficult was the decision to shift my central design focus.

Once I had closed the box and turned on the light, it was a television! Due to the fifties-style rounded corners of the box and the pebble feet, this strange little piece had mutated into something straight out of Bedrock—*not* a look that I typically strive for in my art!

Taken aback, I set it aside. Days and weeks passed and suddenly this area of the state was inundated with flash floods—twice within two weeks, as a result of two hurricanes that made it this far north. Water was everywhere. Streams and rivers tripled in size. After days of moping inside and weathering the rain, I took another look at the box and decided then and there to surrender to its humor. An image of two sullen girls in a rowboat became the new focal point. Their boat was clearly their necessity to stay afloat. I decided to forego my original poem selection and replace it with a simple statement: "Mabel and Ethel set out for high waters." Enough said.

To see more of Nina's artwork, visit:
www.ninabagley.com

Lulu's Girly Get-Up-and-Go

MARTHA LENT

. . . .

I started this project by trying to find the perfect container to fit the theme, "Accessories & Necessities." There seemed to be endless possibilities. I considered using a vintage hatbox, wicker sewing kit or a cosmetic case. I scoured my favorite thrift and antique stores and came up empty-handed. I decided to try eBay for the first time and quickly became addicted! I found so many yummy treats, it was hard to decide. I ended up choosing a very special silver hat-box. I was inspired by its nice oval shape, pretty silver color and cute little airplane graphic on the top.

The next challenge was to figure out what would go inside, again . . . so many choices. I jotted down my list of ideas and made some design sketches, while still considering the central theme of the project.

Then it came to me . . . "Ah ha! What does a girl need most? A purse, hat, really cute shoes and of course, pink lipstick!"

Next, I shopped. Then shopped some more. I found the shoes, hat and mirror at one store, the vintage purse at an antique mall and a variety of really beautiful handmade papers from The Paper Source. In my arsenal of stuff at home I have different colors of rickrack, assorted kinds of acrylic and enamel paint, beads and several foam paint daubers, which I often use for making dots. I painted the inside of the box my favorite lime green, lined the lid with some delightful paper, added rickrack and black sassy tassels to the shoes and purse and embellished the outside of the hat box with blue dots. The final touches came by adding the mirror to the inside of the lid, placing pink heart beads around its perimeter and making flowers out of all the lovely paper I bought. I used a craft knife to carefully cut out the flower design from one of the papers to mount on the top and side of the box, just to give it that extra kick. The lid is functional and will hang up as you check your look . . . before you get up and go!

To see more of Martha's artwork, visit:
www.MarthaLentStudios.com

Dress-Up Girl

LYNN WHIPPLE

· ·

The first trick was to find an interesting case to "alter," though I didn't have to go much farther than my stuff-filled studio, kind of like Dorothy in her own back yard. I had been saving a wonderful doll case that had a picture of Cinderella and Prince Charming on the cover and pictures of circus animals on the inside. I am not even sure what it was used for, but it was the perfect size and character for something . . . now to figure out what it wanted to be.

In thinking about the classic story of Cinderella, I remembered the part where her fairy godmother whips up this amazing gown for her to wear to the ball. I loved that part of the story about as much as I loved playing dress-up as a girl. So there was the beginning of my idea. I decided to make the case into a special closet that was especially intended for playing dress up.

I began by finding an old photo that could have been me in the 1800s, at age 6 or so, and collaging it on the cover of the "closet." The next step was to cover the area all around the photo with white and decorate it in my way, to make it tell my story. I have a thing for the color red. I used it on the front and again in stripes on the sides. It was starting to take shape! I collaged the inside, aged it a bit, and continued the red stripes around the inside edges. It was feeling the way I hoped.

Now that I had a great case . . . I wanted to look inside and find a surprise. The logical thing was to put an accessory inside to play dress-up with! I had just received three wonderful muslin dresses in the mail from an artist-friend that were perfect. I altered one and dipped it in bee's wax and it fit! Sometimes things work out right off the bat and it's magic.

I think, sometimes, one of the hardest things is to come up with a title for a piece. In this "case," I think I will call it "Dress-Up Girl." Enjoy!

To see more of Lynn's artwork, visit:
www.whippleart.com

Flight Attendant, Mindy

CLAUDINE HELLMUTH

Once the theme was decided, I didn't have an idea right away. I had a vague concept, which I liked—the thought that Accessories *are* Necessities. For some of us girls, things like shoes and purses are not only accessories, they are absolute necessities. I liked the campy imagery that this twist on the theme conjured up. I thought of colorful shoes and purses, but I didn't have a firm idea how the project might take shape. I needed to find my suitcase before any real planning could begin.

When I first got my case, I loved the shape and form, but I had no idea of the imagery that I wanted to create. Where to start? I gave it a coat of gesso as a base coat. It helped me to look at it as a clean slate. While applying the gesso to the surface, the shape of the case reminded me of a doll that I had when I was little. It was a doll head and torso that you could apply makeup to and fix her hair and, best of all—it came in a case with all her accessories.

I thought, "Yes! That is it! I will make this a *poppet doll and accessory case* with a giant poppet doll and all the trimmings." Now that I had an idea, I was off and running. I began by painting the outside of the case pink and the inside a light blue. While I let it dry I created a large poppet doll.

Now for the accessories! The first hat I created was a pillbox hat out of watercolor paper. When I held it up to her head she looked like a flight attendant. Then another idea started forming. How about a flight attendant and all the accessories that she needed to take on her trips? I named her Mindy.

I created various other hats and purses and even eyeglasses. I added a velcro tab to Mindy's hairline and one on each hat so that they could easily be switched out. I made a very small slit near her ear with a craft knife so that the glasses could slide on. I was on a roll! I was having so much fun I had to force myself to stop making accessories.

As a finishing touch, I glued a feather boa to the bottom of the case and buttons on the outside in various shades of pink.

I never thought that my project was going to turn out this way, but that was the joy of it. By allowing each idea to lead to the next, I found myself caught up in a wild adventure and enjoying every minute of it.

Gallery

HE DREAMED OF PINK SPOTTED HORSES AND OF HOME... In this collage I used the sketching in paint technique. First I painted the entire canvas a light blue. After that was dry I painted white acrylic paint on top and drew into the paint.

GARY DIDN'T REALIZE HALLOWEEN WAS LAST WEEK... After painting the canvas a dark teal, I layered white tissue paper into the wet paint and then gave it a wash with more teal paint to enhance the texture. I added the collage elements and did the line drawing using a small brush and white acrylic paint.

TALK, GOSSIP, SPECULATION ...I began this assemblage by painting the cigar box light blue. I found a school image of a group of women together, copied it and glued it to water color paper using gel medium. I created hats for each of the women and secured the piece to the cigar box using wooden spools. As a finishing touch I painted the sides of the cigar box pink, and I added xerography print words (enlarged from text found in a book) to a piece of acrylic for the lid.

COMPANION ... This piece uses masking tape and sketching in wet paint in a subtle way. You don't have to have a lot of texture in your collage backgrounds to create interest. Sometimes a hint of texture is all you need.

BILL DOESN'T LIKE WAFFLES ...I began this collage by painting the canvas light yellow. I marked where I thought I would like my book to go, and created an unstretched canvas book like the one that I did on page 76. I added the blue polka dots by dipping the end of my brush in paint and dabbing it on the canvas. The pen and ink words were added by writing with my left (nondominant) hand to create a child-like handwriting look. I copied the text out of a marriage handbook from 1938.

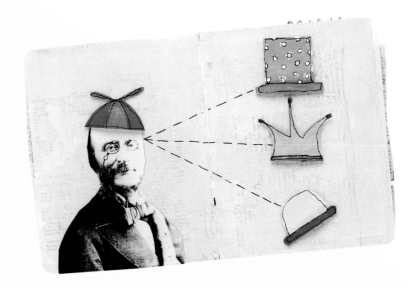

MAY I GET YOU SOMETHING FROM THE KITCHEN?
...I began this piece by creating a xerography print of the figure using brown oil paint on watercolor paper. After that I painted the canvas yellow and trimmed scrapbook paper into the shape of the house. I added a crown and buttons to my figure and as a finishing touch a bit of text cut from an old romance novel saying. A domestic diva was born!

MAN WITH 4 HATS ...I prepared for this piece by sanding and gessoing a children's board book. Next, I layered tissue paper and text from and old book in the background. I painted over the papers with light green and drew into it with a pencil. After I chose my main figure, I thought it would be fun to give him interchangeable hats. I created the hats using paint and ink pen on a sheet of canvas pad and after I cut them out I secured them to the book using Velcro tabs. After adding a tab to the man's forehead, I could change out his hats!

SHE HAD LUCK IN GOLF, IT MADE ALL THE MEN CRAZY
...I began this collage by painting the entire background a light teal blue and layering white tissue into the wet paint. I sketched into the wet paint using a pencil. Once everything was dry, I added clouds using contact paper shapes and Titan Buff. I found funny text from an old 1936 golfing manual, and I used it to jump-start the theme for the figure in the piece.

GETTING READY...After covering the pages with gesso, I layered on white tissue paper and while everything was still wet, I added line drawings into the wet paint using pencil. I trimmed the middle pages so they would be shorter than the other pages and cut them into three sections. I added a figure of the woman in the background and then again on the flaps that I created giving her different shoes, shirts and pants on each of the flaps so I could change her outfit by moving them. The wonderful thing about altered books is that it's very easy to add interactive parts.

THE SNOW BIRD...After painting the cigar box a dark midnight blue, I added snow in the background by dipping a small brush handle into paint and then dabbing it onto the back of the box. I cut my figure out and glued her onto watercolor paper. After it was all dry I added an Elmer's Glue crackle to the body of the figure. I cut out a rectangle in the middle of her torso and slipped in a plastic doll-house window. For finishing touches I added a red house that peeks through her chest and also a tree and red bird in the background.

RESOURCES

Collage Supply Sources
ArtChix Studio
sheets of antique photos
www.artchixstudio.com

ARTitude
sheets of vintage photos
www.artitudezine.com

ArtSafe images
royalty-free contemporary images
www.cre8it.com

Collage Joy
vintage collage, assemblage supplies
www.collagejoy.com

The Cre8tive Eye Studio
*great images (proceeds benefit a
no-kill animal rescue)*
www.picturetrail.com/thecre8tivei

Dover Publications
(Pictorial Archive Series)
series contains copyright-free images
www.doverpublications.com

Ebay.com
*(search listings for vintage papers
and photos)*
www.ebay.com

Found Elements
general collage materials
www.foundelements.com

Instant Inspiration
collage packets, vintage ephemera
www.greatstuff4you.com

KLOJ
packets of antique papers, elements
www.kloj.com

Lost Aussie Designs
unique images ready for collage
www.lostaussie.com

MantoFev
packets of collage supplies
www.mantofev.com

Rubber Baby Buggy Bumpers
collage sheets, rubber stamps
www.rubberbaby.com

Tuscan Rose
general collage supplies
www.tuscanrose.com

Art Supply Sources
Golden Artist Colors
acrylic paints, mediums
www.goldenpaints.com

Loew-Cornell
brushes
www.loew-cornell.com

InspirationalPublications
Art Calendar Magazine
www.artcalendar.com

ARTitude
www.artitudezine.com

Arttella Words and Art
www.artellawordsandart.com

cloth paper scissors
www.clothpaperscissors.com

Dog Eared Magazine
www.dogearedmagazine.com

Expression Magazine
www.expressionartmagazine.com

The Gleaner
http://groups.yahoo.com/group/TheGleane
rZine

IN(ner) Question
http://moderngypsy.com/iq/

New American Paintings
www.newamericanpaintings.com

quilting arts magazine
www.quiltingarts.com

ReadyMade
www.readymademag.com

Somerset Studio Magazine
www.somersetstudio.com

StudioNOTES
www.studionotes.org

TubLeggs
www.bonkersfiber.com/sale/tublegs/tuble
gs.html

Collage & Assemblage Artists
Visit my links page at
www.collageartist.com/links.htm
for a list of artists' Web sites.
Inspiration that is not to be missed!

INDEX

CONTINUE YOUR CREATIVE JOURNEY
WITH THESE FINE NORTH LIGHT BOOKS!

Collage Discovery Workshop
Claudine Hellmuth

Discover innovative techniques and demonstrations specifically designed to achieve the modern, eclectic collage effect that has become so popular today. Claudine Hellmuth will introduce you to the basics of collage. You'll explore techniques such as heat transfers, peeling paper, wax stamping, rusting metal and more as you are lead through a series of creative exercises that are sure to ignite the creative spark in every crafter!

ISBN 1-58180-343-5   paperback   128 pages   #32313-K

Art to Wear
Jana Ewy

There's no better way to show off your creative talents than to adorn yourself, your family and friends with your own works of art. Whatever your unique style, this book shows you how to create jewelry, accessories and clothing that match your personality. Author Jana Ewy demonstrates how to dress up jackets, sweaters, t-shirts, flip-flops, purses and belts with paint, ink, metal, fabric, fibers, beads and even Chinese coins. You'll be inspired to make your mark on your clothing and accessories by the over 25 projects and variations included in the book.

ISBN 1-58180-597-7   paperback   96 pages   #33110-K

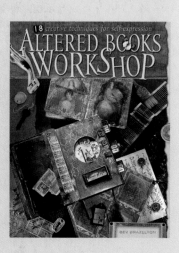

Altered Books Workshop
Bev Brazelton

A book isn't just a book anymore—it can have windows, doors, drawers and more. *Altered Books Workshop* gives you comprehensive instruction and inspiration for creating multi-dimensional art that is a reflection of your moods, thoughts and life. You'll learn how to turn old books into dazzling works of art by combining mixed media and papercrafting techniques with elements of collaging, journaling, rubber stamping and scrapbooking. You'll love learning the wide range of creative techniques for crafting unique, personalized altered books offered through the over 50 projects and ideas inside *Altered Books Workshop*.

ISBN 1-58180-535-7   paperback   128 pages   #32889-K

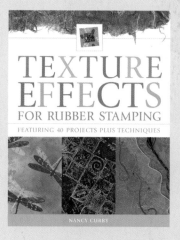

Texture Effects for Rubber Stamping
Nancy Curry

Crafters can satisfy their craving for texture with this treasure trove of 37 elegant card and gift projects. Inside, you'll find an abundance of texture-making techniques, including stamping with metallic paints, resist effects, alcohol inks, layers of acetate, watercolors and embellishments. Even better, this book is about more than just cards—there are also fresh ideas for turning ordinary boxes, tags, clocks and tiles into memorable gift items. *Texture Effects for Rubber Stamping* is an inspirational resource that crafters will turn to time after time for ideas and instruction.

ISBN 1-58180-558-6   paperback   128 pages   33014-K